35

Islam and America

Islam and America

Building a Future without Prejudice

Anouar Majid

ROWMAN & LITTLEFIELD PUBLISHERS, INC.
Lanham • Boulder • New York • Toronto • Plymouth, UK

Published by Rowman & Littlefield Publishers, Inc.
A wholly owned subsidiary of The Rowman & Littlefield Publishing Group, Inc.
4501 Forbes Boulevard, Suite 200, Lanham, Maryland 20706
http://www.rowmanlittlefield.com

Estover Road, Plymouth PL6 7PY, United Kingdom

British Library Cataloguing in Publication Information Available

Library of Congress Cataloging-in-Publication Data

Majid, Anouar, 1960–
    Islam and America : building a future without prejudice / Anouar Majid.
        p. cm.
    ISBN 978-1-4422-1412-5 (cloth : alk. paper) — ISBN 978-1-4422-1414-9
(electronic)
    1. Islam—United States—Public opinion. 2. Islam—United States—
History. 3. Islam—21st century. 4. Islamic civilization. 5. United
States—Civilization. 6. East and West. I. Title.
    BP67.U6M35 2012
    297.0973—dc23   2011047088

⊗ ™ The paper used in this publication meets the minimum requirements of
American National Standard for Information Sciences—Permanence of Paper
for Printed Library Materials, ANSI/NISO Z39.48-1992.

Printed in the United States of America

Contents

Preface

I have long felt that non-Muslim Americans and non-American Muslims needed an accessible resource that would help them understand why the United States and Muslim-majority nations are trapped in a seemingly endless conflict. Excellent books on Islam and the United States abound, but such studies have not managed to alter the course of the torturous encounter between America and the world of Islam. Despite an overflow of publications on the two civilizations, we are nowhere near the kind of understanding that would help us make a real difference. Often, it seems as if we were drowning in information, not being rescued by it.

This book, therefore, is not meant to be a scholarly contribution to the fields of Islamic and American studies. I am far less interested in unearthing new historical information (or in compiling it) than in offering a new perspective that may help Americans and Muslims to think differently about their troubled relationship. I use my own experiences as a Muslim-born American from Morocco and rely on the information made available to us by a select group of scholars to make sense of American-Muslim relations throughout the centuries. The goal is not to speak a party line—liberal, conservative, religious, or otherwise—but to trace the underlying challenges to a better understanding and future for both peoples. This is not a light matter: American presidents have been trying to reach out to Muslims and change their perceptions of America since the terrorist attacks of September 11, 2001. Unfortunately, there has been very little change, if at all, in attitudes. President George W. Bush and his hawkish cabinet have been replaced by the somewhat more liberal administration of Barack Obama; Osama bin Laden and several of his henchmen are dead; uprisings in Tunisia, Egypt, and Libya have toppled governments and demonstrations in other parts of the Arab world are leading to a wholesale rethinking of the future of Arabs and Muslims; yet, it would be safe to predict that by the time this book is published there will still be little understanding between most Americans and Muslims. That is because our vision of the future remains undermined by deeply embedded prejudices inherited from the past. Understand, though, we must, if only because nothing less than our collective human future is at stake. We need to be brave enough to find solutions, however unpalatable they may taste to us, if we want to bequeath a better world to our descendants.

As the reader will gather from the Introduction, I couldn't start a project like this without explaining to people who have grown skeptical of, or even given up on, America, why the world's mightiest nation can still help Muslims work out their dilemmas. Many Muslims, like many people around the world, tend to view the United States as a voracious empire intent on ravaging other people's lands and cultures to satisfy its seemingly insatiable appetite for natural resources. They watch American shows and conclude that the nation has no moral compass left. While there is no shortage of critics—foreign and domestic—bemoaning the ill effects of consumer culture on American society, or condemning America's unwise military outreach, the United States stands on a more solid foundation, one that is liberating not just to its citizens, but also to the entire world. The republic designed by a band of revolutionaries in the eighteenth century may be severely challenged today, but it endures in a thousand different ways. More than that, we must do everything in our power to preserve it. The United States, as envisioned by its founders, is a precious gift to the world and human civilization. America may appear to be hostile to Islam, but it is, without a doubt, the best place on Earth for Muslims to flourish.

It helps to have an appreciation of the historic and cultural significance of the United States before going back to the past to see how the current tensions between the United States and the Islamic world are built on a long history of prejudice and narrowly defined self-interest on one side, and the stagnation of Islamic societies on the other. For America, Islam has always appeared to be a fraudulent faith, one that needed to be cast away and replaced with American

Christianity. For Muslims, America, much like the Christian West, now seems to embody the face or arrogance and colonialism.

Because of this charged atmosphere, neither culture has been able to appreciate the contributions of the other to its own history, for both civilizations—American and Muslim—are more deeply intertwined than cultural purists on both sides care to acknowledge. Without Muslim and Arab contributions, America wouldn't be what it is today; and without America's good works in the Middle East, the region would be far worse than it is now. A reassessment of American–Muslim relations in the past is, therefore, indispensable for a realistic dialogue, which is the only way to build trust. Just as was the case with Native Americans, Americans must become aware of their long-held prejudices against Muslims, while Muslims, departing from their familiar pattern of blaming the West and America, must acknowledge their stagnation and rethink their own assumptions and prejudices. This is the only way to overcome the debilitating impasse in America's encounter with Islam, which is bound to continue in the age of economic globalization.

The foundations of a genuine, productive dialogue between the United States and the Islamic world, including Arabs, must be delineated through an honest look at the prejudices America has harbored about Islam and Arabs for so long. Categories like Muslim and Arab tend to be complicated and sometimes confusing because an Arab is not necessarily a Muslim, and a Muslim is not exclusively Arab. In fact, Arabs make up a mere minority in the vast world of Muslim-majority nations, which stretches from Africa to East Asia, and could not possibly represent the rich cultural traditions of the entire world of Islam. However, since this book deals with the United States and Islam, the center stage of this historic encounter has been in what we nowadays call the Middle East, which, with few exceptions, like Iran and Turkey, is mostly Arab. The Middle East has had more of a claim on the American imagination than Muslim-majority nations like Senegal, Mali, or Bangladesh.

By the same token, I am assuming Arabs to be part of the Islamic fabric, even when many Arabs are actually Christian, not Muslim. The overwhelming majority of the Arab world's population is Muslim, and Arab culture is heavily imprinted by the Islamic legacy. The Arabic language and the Islamic religion have always been intertwined. "In almost all those Arab countries that have written constitutions," wrote the historian Bernard Lewis in his 2010 book,

Faith and Power: Religion and Politics in the Middle East, "Islam figures either as the religion of the state or as the 'principal source of legislation.'"[1] In any case, America's reassessment of its bias against Islam (in the imprecise sense used here) is necessary if only to allow American policy makers and cultural ambassadors to realize that they are not only going against Muslim cultures struggling to carve out a respectable place in the global scene, but that they themselves are the product of a culture that has had a persistently negative image of Islam and Muslims.

Because America was first imagined as a Christian nation, a new Zion, and the Pilgrims as Israelites seeking refuge from tyranny, Islam, as it had long been in the European Christian tradition, became the every antithesis of the new Promised Land. Christian America's strong anti-Muslim sentiments were not radically changed even when the American Revolution, inspired by the philosophies of the Enlightenment, lowered the tempo of earlier religious zealotry. Islam, in this period, became the prototype of tyranny, an epithet to be thrown at political rivals, new religions, or even new fashions. Charitable views of Islam, particularly on the religion's better treatment of slaves and blacks, were expressed; but as the nineteenth century wore on and American missionaries fanned out to convert both Muslims and Christians in the Middle East, older anti-Islamic motifs, combined with millennial beliefs, such as the imperative of restoring Jews to the Holy Land before the return of the messiah, turned Muslims into either satanic figures or hopelessly primitive people to be disposed of. America had spent a great deal of the nineteenth and early twentieth centuries literally building the Arab world (a fact still not widely known today), but US dependence on Islamic oil and the rise of a new brand of Protestant fundamentalism only exacerbated the cultural divide. To engage Muslims in a meaningful dialogue, the United States would have, then, to take stock of this charged history and appeal to its better traditions of democracy and respect for other nations in order to help Muslims overcome their long, debilitating cultural stagnation.

Although many of the Christian polemical views about Islam are nothing more than religious diatribes—part of the religious war that has been going on for centuries between Christianity and Islam—the recurring charge that Muslims live in despotic societies and that they have fallen behind most of the great civilizations of the world, in terms of development and intellectual renewal, needs to be taken seriously. For, as self-righteous as the statements of a succession of American leaders—stretching from Thomas Jefferson to Barack Obama—regarding the lack of freedom in Muslim societies may have been, they do contain an element of truth, one that is fitfully being recognized by Muslim thinkers today. Muslims have spent a great amount of time embellishing their traditions, painting their bloody history, full of political assassinations, violence, and narrow-minded literalism, into one long golden age of triumphs and unmatched achievements that all came to a screeching halt with Western incursions in the modern period. This is a dangerously misleading reading of the history of the Islamic world and thought, one that must be reassessed to better enable Muslims to participate more fully in our global civilization.

Just as Americans have long been blinded to the realities of Muslim societies through their attachment to biblical geographies and truths, so have Muslims been trapped in a belief system that prevented them from becoming equal partners in the making of contemporary civilization. Western belligerence only exacerbated this Islamic deficit since occupation and exploitation invariably lead to the hardening of fundamentalist and obscurantist tendencies. It therefore behooves the United States to engage Muslims with respect and fairness, if the Islamic world is to confront its own myths and step out confidently into the global arena without delusions of grandeur or debilitating pangs of inferiority.

One way for the two nations to move ahead in a new millennial tradition of hope is to gain a better appreciation of their respective accomplishments to the common stock of human civilization. Although Muslim rulers closed the path to philosophical inquiry by the twelfth century, Islam has contributed significantly to the making of the modern West, and is, in fact, part of the fabric of American culture in ways that are not always obvious to average Americans. That a man of Islamic heritage was elected president of the United States in 2008 is part of this long, often obscure, legacy. Islam, in this sense, is not the antithesis of the West but an inextricable part of its foundation and culture. By the same token, Muslims and Arabs need to have a better appreciation of the role the United States played in building the modern nations of the Middle East. The universities and armies Americans helped develop were, in some ways, the foundations of Arab nationalism. American missionaries in the region were advocates of local cultures with their government. Highlighting these histories would give more depth and meaning to a new American–Muslim relationship.

Despite its shortcomings, America, the expression of an earth-shattering revolution, remains an inspiration to the whole world, including the Islamic one. Muslims could aspire to a similar role in modern history, but they need to recalibrate their approach and assumptions in order to better convey their ideals and inspire future generations of Muslims. As the international singer Bono wrote in October 2009, "the world wants to believe in America again." The world, he continued, needs America's ideas "at a time when the rest of the world is running out of them."[2]

As with the Israeli–Palestinian conflict or the Jewish–Muslim contretemps, only trust built through an awareness of common histories and cultural traditions, not political sloganeering or public-relations spinning, could give birth to the long-awaited period of peace and prosperity in the Islamic world and the Middle East. There is no end to the supply of grievances, if that is what we want to look for. There are no saints in the history of nations, only conquerors and conquered, winners and losers, survivors and victims. Nations change hands, maps are drawn and redrawn, histories are rewritten, and monotheistic religions clash because they all claim to have privileged access to God's words. Palestinians may feel unjustly treated today, but the Jews have been persecuted and dispossessed for thousands of years, including by Arabs and Muslims. Both Jews and Palestinians are victims of ancient prejudices or redeeming nationalist schemes. We have invested and reinvested the tired land of Palestine with too many fables and myths and condemned its people—Jews, Christians, Muslims, and others—to lives of endless turmoil. Palestine is really no more than an average land on which people have projected their fantasies across the millennia.

Americans, too, are caught up in an impossible race to power and domination. We may overpower any nation today, but we can't, in the end, defy the unsentimental march of history. The Mediterranean basin, which framed my horizon when I was growing up in Tangier, is ringed by once glorious and powerful nations who have long accommodated themselves to the cycles of birth, decline, and rebirth. Nothing, our elders told us repeatedly, lasts forever or stays the same.

Such awareness, though, is not a call for resignation. We all—Americans and Muslims, Israelis and Palestinians—must rediscover the promise of the Enlightenment, whose core revolutionary principles—the banishment of ignorance and prejudice, the elevation of reason over blind faith, the quest for a just society that is fulfilling to all, and the uncompromising dedication to human dignity—were snuffed out too early and prematurely. It will take time to replace pessimism with hope, suspicion with genuine openness, and clashes with alliances; but we are better off starting now than delaying good works to some indefinite time in the future.

This preface sketches the book's main themes. Following the introduction on why America matters to Muslims and the world, we will embark on a whirlwind, if not bumpy, tour of American–Muslim relations and prejudices in the first three chapters. Through the use of quotations, we will be able to hear many voices from the past in order gauge the extent to which attitudes have changed or remained the same over decades and centuries. Such quotations produce an echo chamber of sorts, helping us sense, in a palpable way, how our language and views have remained remarkably stable throughout history. Once we have a sense of that past, we will look at Islam and America briefly and critically before we think about what needs to be altered. I don't, however, offer any concrete blueprints because I believe that we must first agree on whether our old habits are the main cause of our discord and vexations. People need to be convinced that the ancient regimes that govern their lives and shape their thoughts and emotions have outlived their usefulness and are, in fact, hampering the search for a better human civilization. That is what America's Founding Fathers did. They knew the time had come for a radical change, a new beginning, and so they severed ties with the mother country and built a new nation. The world, as we all know by now, has never been the same.

I have been reading and writing on Islam and America for close to a decade now, but in putting this book together, I chose to put aside much of my previous work and rely for most of my information on the part dealing with American–Muslim relations—whether such relations were tinged with religious or secular bias—on a short list of mostly recently published studies. The most comprehensive of these is Michael B. Oren's *Power, Faith, and Fantasy: America in the Middle East, 1776 to the Present* (2007).[3] Oren's widely acclaimed book is not only a fascinating page-turner, but the book covers just about every facet of the American republic's encounter with Arabs.

Without Oren's book, there would have been many historical gaps in my account.

Another invaluable book I read while wrapping up the first draft of my manuscript is Ussama Makdisi's *Faith Misplaced: The Broken Promise of US–Arab Relations: 1820–2001* (2010),[4] an excellent sequel to his equally illuminating *Artillery of Heaven: American Missionaries and the Failed Conversion of the Middle East* (2008).[5] Oren and Makdisi approach the subject from different ideological angles, but their books provide an almost inexhaustible amount of information on American–Arab or American–Muslim relations.

Other studies that are indispensable to our understanding of how the image of Islam in American thought affects US–Muslim relations include Fuad Sha'ban's *Islam and Arabs in Early American Thought: The Roots of Orientalism in America* (1990)[6] and *For Zion's Sake: The Judeo-Christian Tradition in America* (2005);[7] Timothy Marr's *The Cultural Roots of American Islamicism* (2006);[8] Thomas S. Kidd's *American Christians and Islam: Evangelical Culture and Muslims from the Colonial Period to the Age of Terrorism* (2009);[9] Jonathan Curiel's *Al' America: Travels through America's Arab and Islamic Roots* (2008);[10] and, most importantly to me, Robert J. Allison's *The Crescent Obscured: The United States and the Muslim World, 1776–1815* (first published in 1995).[11] It was Allison's pioneering book that lit my interest in American–Muslim relations and opened whole new vistas of inquiry to me. *The Crescent Obscured*, moreover, led me to discover a man who embodies the best of American traditions: erudition, humility, generosity, and tireless dedication to family, friends, and community.

I have had the good fortune of reviewing a number of the titles listed above. I discussed Oren's *Power, Faith, and Fantasy* and Brian Yothers' *The Romance of the Holy Land in American Travel Writing, 1790–1876* (2007),[12] together with other works, in a review essay titled "The Political Geography of Holiness," published in *American Literary History* (2009).[13] I also reviewed Marr's *The Cultural Roots of American Islamicism* for *The Historian* (Spring 2008)[14] and Kidd's *American Christians and Islam* for *Reviews in American History* (June 2009).[15] Much earlier in my study of the subject of Islam and America, I reviewed Allison's *The Crescent Obscured* for the *Journal of American Studies of Turkey* (Spring 1998).[16] Other books that I reviewed include Brian Edwards' *Morocco Bound: Disorienting America's Maghreb, From Casablanca to the Marrakech Express*

(2005)[17] for *Tingis*, the magazine I cofounded and edited until 2010. Portions of these reviews may reappear in different parts of the first few chapters, along with long passages from my article, "Living With Islam," which was published in the *Chronicle of Higher Education* on March 14, 2003.[18] I am grateful to these journals and periodicals for giving me the opportunity to write for them and allowing me to reprint parts of my reviews and articles in this book.

Although they are not mentioned as frequently as the first group of authors, I also learned a great deal from the superb works of Rashid Khalidi, Juan Cole, Paul Baepler, Lotfi Ben Rejeb, Frank Lambert, Elizabeth Boosahda, and Sarah M. A. Gualtieri (whose book on early Arab immigration to the United States I reviewed for the *Journal of American History*), as well as from the epic histories of James A. Field, Jr. and Walter A. McDougall. Field's *From Gibraltar to the Middle East: America and the Mediterranean World, 1776–1882* (first published in 1969 and reissued in 1991)[19] must surely be the indispensable reference to anyone studying America's encounter with Arabs and Muslims in the nineteenth century or even beyond. These sources are bolstered by the excellent work of other historians, intellectuals, and writers who deal with the subjects of Christian Zionism, Islam, America, or Israel. Readers who want more detailed information on any topic touched upon in this book should certainly consult their works. Most of their studies are of the highest scholarly order and are extensively documented.

I am deeply indebted to all the scholars cited in this book for helping me draw a concise picture of the past in order to show why old beliefs have long outlived their usefulness and propose (however tentatively) what radical steps need to be taken for more humane relations. I am also grateful to my editor, Sarah Stanton, who engaged me in a lengthy conversation about the project and gently encouraged me to make significant structural changes in my manuscript that made my views and opinions clearer and more accessible. She knew that the topic might generate strong frustrations among readers, but that didn't deter her at all.

It would have been difficult to write this book while trying to run a new humanities center and globalize my university's agenda without the exciting and creative leadership of Danielle Ripich, the longstanding encouragement of Jacque Carter, the unfailing support of Neal Jandreau and Elizabeth Bennett, the constant generosity of my friend and colleague David Smith, the patience of my wife

Melissa, and the hope my children Ridwan, Mounir, Suhail, and Safia never cease to give me. Many other family members, friends, and colleagues in the United States, Morocco, and Europe have inspired me to keep thinking, talking, and writing. To them all, my heartfelt thanks.

I would feel tremendously accomplished if this modest volume manages to start a new kind of conversation, one that might—if prejudices are kept at bay—help Americans and Muslims get closer to each other. I am fully aware that this is not an easy task, not least because we may all be invited to consider options that may not suit our ideological or religious convictions. It may be helpful to remember, however, that real conversations are, by definition, open-ended and inconclusive. They are sustained by doubt, uncertainty, and playfulness, as well as by good coffee, tea, or, if not proscribed, by good wine. In any case, conversations humanize us; unyielding certitudes turn us into warring tribes and killing machines.

Introduction:
Why America Matters

The election of Barack Obama to the US presidency in November 2008 renewed the promise of America as a nation dedicated to equal opportunity. Coming some seven years after Muslim terrorists killed and maimed thousands of Americans on US soil, it opened a new chapter in the tortuous American–Muslim dialogue, if, indeed, there ever was one. I listened to President Obama's inaugural address on January 20, 2009 and his first address to a joint session of Congress on February 24, read the transcript of the remarks he made in Turkey during his first overseas trip on the same day I gave a talk about America and Islam at Bard College in New York, and awaited, as did much of the world, his address to the Muslim world in Cairo on June 4 of that same year. In less than five months in office, President Obama was able to identify, in a remarkably succinct way, the causes of discord between the United States and Muslim-majority nations and challenge both communities to take bold action in order to build American–Muslim relations on a new footing.

Like most American presidents, President Obama insisted that his nation is not at war with Islam. This could mean that states with armies don't fight religions but other national armies, terrorist groups, or armed insurgents. From a strictly technical point of view, juxtaposing the United States and Islam may seem like comparing apples to oranges; yet, the fact remains that, since 2001, the US government has expended much time and effort in reaching out to Muslims across the world, including American Muslims. The US government doesn't say it wants to reach out to the citizens of Senegal, Turkey, or Bahrain, but to Muslims, *tout court*, because the

1

assumption has always been that Muslims, wherever they may be, don't seem to have a good appreciation of the United States and its role in the world. One might add that American patriotism is a form of religion, one that is akin, in the passions and loyalties it instills in its citizens, to a monotheistic one. But that discussion, as important as it may be, is not the main focus of this book. Anyone watching the nightly news knows that the United States—not, say, the Methodist Church—is embroiled in some kind of conflict with Muslims.

In his inaugural address, President Obama took stock of his own nation's standing and acknowledged the creeping feeling of helplessness that has seized Americans in the last few decades. There is, he told us that cold winter day, "a sapping of confidence across our land; a nagging fear that America's decline is inevitable, that the next generation must lower its sights." But, as he later added for the benefit of his global audience, America is still ready to lead through the hope it instills in generations of newcomers, the miraculous example of its diversity, and its pursuit of peace and mutual interest in foreign relations, especially with the Muslim world. If America could hold on to its eternal truths, it could renew itself for its own welfare and the benefit of humanity. Because of its exceptional history and powers, the United States, President Obama rightly implied in his address, is more needed around the world today than it ever was in the past.

When Obama addressed Congress the following month, he repeated many of the same themes, including America's abundant reservoir of promise and hope for its citizens and the nations of the world. "As we stand at this crossroads of history," the new president told his fellow lawmakers, "the eyes of all people in all nations are once again upon us, watching to see what we do with this moment, waiting for us to lead." The following day, as if to confirm his conviction, the *New York Times* columnist Thomas Friedman, reporting from Seoul, told us that senior South Korean officials couldn't imagine a world without American leadership. The United States, one official said, "is still No. 1 in military, No. 1 in economy, No. 1 in promoting human rights and No. 1 in idealism. Only the US can lead the world. No other country can. China can't. The E.U. is too divided, and Europe is militarily far behind the U.S. So it is only the United States . . . We have never had a more unipolar world than we have today." South Korea's former ambassador to the United States repeated that there is "no one who can replace America" which, he added, "puts a tremendous burden on the American people to do something positive." As weighty as this responsibility may be, however, the ambassador had no doubt that "Americans, as a people, should realize how many hopes and expectations other people are putting on their shoulders."[1]

The Korean officials are right: the rhetoric of decline doesn't really capture the actual power of the United States and the promise of its future. The country may be lagging behind in a number of social indicators, such as access to health care and Internet broadband; its political culture may have been reduced to cheap morality dramas; its infrastructure may look antiquated when compared to the slick, new structures rising in China or Dubai; but the United States remains the largest economy in the world and the best place for the generation of new ideas and solutions. Its old industrial system may be crumbling, but it leads the way in nanotechnology and biotechnology research.

Its higher education system is, in fact, the envy of the world. American universities are the world's laboratory for major inventions, ranging from the laser and FM radio to Viagra, because of the open, entrepreneurial ethos of Americans, not because politicians have willed the system to be so. No wonder the French are worried about a "brain drain" to the United States and the Iranians covet an education in the country their public officials call the Great Satan. In its race to outpace America, China is tapping into its bottomless coffers to replicate the American higher education model; but the best China can do is copy institutional structures, not adopt the democratic culture that drives Americans or foreign students infused by the American spirit of free inquiry and research. No Asian country can truly adopt the American liberal arts tradition, with its strong emphasis on the humanities, because such an education is inextricably intertwined with the American political culture. If American philosophers like Harvard professor Michael J. Sandel are treated like rock stars in Asia it's because they are nurtured in a tradition of free and critical inquiry, not one of discipline. Not only that, but fraud, the *New York Times* reported in October 2010, is so rampant in the Chinese higher education system that it could hamper that nation's notable progress in a few industries. China and its universities would simply not have the same effect on free, unshackled minds. This explains why Simon Tay, a Singaporean scholar, said, "No one in Asia wants to live in a Chinese-dominated world. There is no Chinese dream to which people aspire."[2]

In fact, the Chinese, like the British and others, continue to be inspired, even awed, by America's ideals. When a Chinese business-man posted a picture of Gary F. Locke, the US ambassador to China, casually carrying a backpack with his six-year-old daughter at a Star-bucks in the Seattle airport in the summer of 2011, the Chinese were amazed at the unpretentiousness of American diplomats, something that is unthinkable in their home country. And if the casualness of the ambassador were not enough, the fact that the US diplomat was himself of Chinese ancestry added even more impact to America's welcoming ethos. Similar sentiments were expressed by Ralph Miliband, Britain's Labor Party's leader, around the same time. Having lived in the United States during parts of his childhood and young adulthood, Miliband, the son of a Marxist scholar, developed an admiration for America's exceptional openness and democratic spirit, which could not be found in his home country.[3]

In his inaugural address, Obama provided a sort of roadmap to both Americans and Muslim-majority nations on how to build a bet-ter future together. Having seen histories of racial hatreds and social prejudice yield to a new culture of hope and possibility in his own country, Obama was all too aware of the heavy weight of the past on the present. "Each country must work through its past," he remarked to the Turkish Parliament. "And reckoning with the past can help us seize a better future." The better angels of the American republic, he seemed to be saying again and again, are worth preserving; but hos-tility and prejudice toward Islam as a faith and religion are not. "The United States is not, and will never be, at war with Islam," President Obama said emphatically. "In fact, our partnership with the Muslim world is critical not just in rolling back the violent ideologies that people of all faiths reject, but also to strengthen opportunity for all its people."

By the time he stood in Cairo University to deliver his much-awaited keynote address on Islam, Obama vowed to defend the rights of his Muslim citizens who had done much to build his nation, but he also called on Muslims not to succumb to crude stereotypes of America as a mere "self-interested empire." The United States, a nation born out of a revolution against tyranny, has given the world new hope, Obama said, and it could certainly continue to do so. With its unshakeable commitment to Israel, his government would still push for an independent state for the Palestinians; repair America's historical mistakes toward Iran; and encourage religious freedom, women's rights, economic development, education, democracy, and pluralism across the Muslim world. These are all necessary conditions for better American–Muslim relations, Obama suggested. "But," the president warned, "if we choose to be bound by the past, we will never move forward."

Before we trace the conflicted history between America and Islam from the colonial period to the present, I must first add my conviction, with Obama, the South Korean officials, and the scholar Simon Tay, that America, despite its many shortcomings, remains a beacon of hope for Muslims and non-Muslims alike. Many Arabs and Muslims, as the award-winning historian Ussama Makdisi has shown in *Faith Misplaced*, have grown so disillusioned with America's enormous political faux pas and betrayal of its own ideals in the Middle East that they have lost faith in its progressive promise.[4] And yet, America's language of freedom continues to inspire Arabs and Muslims as it had more than a century ago. The dispatches of US diplomats revealed by WikiLeaks in 2010 reflected American values at their best. The Americans could barely conceal their contempt for the obscene levels of corruption in all the countries they reported on, including Tunisia and Egypt. The US government may have upheld Tunisia's president Zine el Abidine ben Ali's regime for decades to protect its economic interests and contain Islamic extremism, but it was the American diplomats' reports on corruption among Tunisia's small ruling elite that provided the proof Tunisians needed to spark their revolt. For example, Ambassador Robert F. Godec, writing on July 17, 2009, noted that "many Tunisians are frustrated by the lack of political freedom and angered by First Family corruption, high unemployment and regional inequities." Of course, the ambassador noted that "Tunisians have been deeply angry over the war in Iraq and perceived US bias towards Israel," but, he reported, "most still admire the . . . American dream" and "wish for more educational and scientific exchanges, and a belief in the American culture of innovation. Tunisians," continued the US ambassador, "see these as important for their future."[5]

Before the outbreak of Arab demonstrations, President Obama had been worried about the future of the region and had commissioned a report on how best to transition the region to a more democratic system. He was not on the side of Arab autocrats, partly because it was no longer in America's best interest to be. American technology powerhouses like Google and Facebook, in concert with US-funded organizations, had coached leading Arab activists on how to use their technologies to implement social change in their home countries before the outbreak of the uprisings. Arab leaders like Hosni Mubarak complained about American interference in their domestic affairs, but, given the silence of the Arab and Muslim masses on the matter, it appears as if Arabs and Muslims do not object to American-inspired regime change that empowers them. When Arab or Muslims autocrats tried to disable Internet networks during the uprisings of 2011, young American idealists huddled together in Washington, D.C. to devise new technologies that would help the communication systems of Arab and Muslim democrats elude the grasp of authoritarian regimes.[6] As was made abundantly clear in his Mideast speech of May 19, 2011, President Obama was, in the end, on the side of Mohammed Bouazizi, the Tunisian street vendor who sparked the Tunisian and Arab revolutions after he had set himself ablaze on December 17, 2010, in protest against rampant injustice.

American history provided its share of inspiration, too. Arabic-speaking and Francophone Tunisian protesters carried homemade placards in English saying "Freedom," "I Have a Dream. Une Tunisie Libre," and "Game Over." They shouted "Yes, we can." During this episode, President Obama expressed admiration for the Tunisian rebels when he affirmed that "the United States stands with the entire international community in bearing witness to this brave and determined struggle for the universal rights that we must all uphold, and we will long remember the images of the Tunisian people seeking to make their voices heard."[7]

On the day before the Tunisian president fled his country, Hillary Clinton, the US Secretary of State, chastised Arab leaders in Qatar, telling them that their nations were "sinking in the sand" because of corruption and tyranny. Even on the question of Palestine, Secretary Clinton could claim the upper hand by reminding Arabs that—rhetoric notwithstanding—the United States was the top financial donor to the Palestinian Authority.

When the Tunisian revolt moved to Egypt, I saw people holding signs stating "Freedom" and "Yes we can, too," while President Obama reiterated that he was for peaceful demonstrations and that President Hosni Mubarak and his government had no option but to be on the side of freedom, democracy, and human rights. "The people of Egypt," President Obama said in his weekly radio address of January 28, 2011, "have rights that are universal. That includes the right to peaceful assembly and association, the right to free speech, and the ability to determine their own destiny. These are human rights. And the United States will stand up for them everywhere." Despite lingering worries about the possible rise of Islamism, President Obama praised the Egyptian revolution after the ouster of President Hosni Mubarak and noted that "it was the moral force of nonviolence—not terrorism and mindless killing—that bent the arc of history toward justice once more." The legacy of American freedom was not absent in the Egyptian revolution. An Egyptian businessman told Nicholas Kristof, the *New York Times* columnist, that American people "are pioneers. We want to be like them." Then the Egyptian asked: "Is that a crime?"[8]

Because America continues to inspire people seeking liberty, I am still betting on its power to help remake the world. The United States is not just another country. Its birth inaugurated far-reaching changes in human consciousness. Its people and revolution have engendered a brave new world of freedom and possibility, even as the excessive acquisitiveness of its barons and the seemingly insatiable appetite of its commercial interests continue to sap at its glorious legacy. "Our country has been the first to prove to the world two truths the most salutary to human society," Thomas Jefferson wrote in 1820, "that man can govern himself, and that religious freedom is the most effective anodyne against religious dissension." The visionary Founding Father was suggesting that pluralism and diversity are the very lifeblood of a stable democratic system because, unlike in religion, the true principle of civil government is "divided we stand, united we fall."[9] President Obama reiterated the same principles when he addressed Indonesians and Muslims from Jakarta on November 10, 2010, seventeen months after his Cairo speech. He praised Indonesia's philosophy of "unity in diversity," although a more rigid brand of Islam was, by that time, already making ominous inroads into the liberal culture he had known when he lived there with his mother and Muslim stepfather as a child.[10]

What makes the United States an exceptional place is its system of "divided sovereignties," robust culture of self-reliance, and the astonishing generosity of its people whose voluntary, private charitable donations add up to a quarter-trillion dollars a year—"enough," as one scholar out it, "that the entire national income of any of the Scandinavian countries could be financed entirely through donations." In 2009, despite the severe economic recession that was gripping the country, Americans still gave three hundred billion dollars for charity. And if that were not enough, the following year, forty of America's wealthiest people pledged to give away at least half their fortunes for the same cause, adding another six hundred billion dollars to the fund.[11] One of these philanthropists was New York City Mayor Michael R. Bloomberg, who, during the same week the billionaires' announcement was made, gave a stirring speech in New York City defending Muslims' right to build a Muslim community center, known as Park51, two blocks away from Ground Zero, the site of the Twin Towers that were brought down by Muslim terrorists on September 1, 2001. Mayor Bloomberg did so in the face of growing national hostility to mosque building, not just in New York City, but also across the country.[12]

My personal experiences straddling the Muslim and American worlds convinced me that Americans and Muslims in other parts of the world need to know each other through a cultural understanding that allows for unvarnished truths to be told, not through a set of stereotypes inherited from histories of conflict or through empty platitudes. Just as Islam is mostly seen as an antimodern and violent religion with almost no redeeming qualities, America is almost always read by Muslims as a nation of heartless materialists. If Muslims are religious fanatics, Americans are isolated people without feelings for neighbor or kin. Neither stereotype is true. My experience growing up in Tangier and living in Morocco endowed me with a high appreciation for tolerance and critical inquiry, while my life in the United States has taught me that America very much remains the universal nation and beacon of hope that the celebrated nineteenth-century poet Walt Whitman painted in broad strokes. I have witnessed the stunning generosity of Americans endless times. America very often reveals its capacious self when it is not on public display.

One example that struck me in 2010 was the way Transportation Security Administration (TSA) agents in a small airport in Iowa handled the body search of a head-covered Muslim female. On May 13 of that year, when the United States was still somewhat jittery over the failed bomb attack in New York City by a Pakistani man almost two weeks earlier, I witnessed a series of exchanges at the Waterloo airport in the state of Iowa that captured the complexity of the relationship between the United States and Islam. This airport, which serves the region known for its John Deere industries and the

University of Northern Iowa, is so small that only three daily flights by Delta airlines connected it to the Twin Cities in Minneapolis, and from there to the rest of the country and the world. There were no long lines leading to the luggage scanner section, so I tarried a bit before I decided to have my briefcase checked and walk through the metal detector.

Before I could do so, however, the line suddenly got blocked. A slim, scarf-covered, Arabic-speaking Muslim woman with jeans had triggered some alarm and needed to be inspected more closely, but the young woman and the Muslim man with her refused to allow the male TSA agent guarding the entrance to the gate to touch her. From what I understood, a female agent had to be found. The line at the security checkpoint grew longer, and I could read some impatience on a traveler's face. But throughout the whole stalemate, which was eventually resolved with the help of a female agent, a climate of remarkable civility was maintained. Everyone present, including the few travelers about to board the puddle-jumper, remained discreetly out of the way, making sure that the Muslim travelers, who were accompanied by another young man and a boy, were as comfortable as could be under the circumstances. Maybe it was the solid values of the Midwest at display, but there was no hysteria, no fearful or disapproving looks of any kind, and no private complaints about the whole situation. When the Muslim passengers boarded the small plane, they were greeted with the same smile the rest of the passengers received.

Episodes like this have always captured my attention because, at some level, they take place in normal, average circumstances, away from the sensational eyes of the media and politics. One gets to feel the real core of America at such settings. The civility shown the Muslims at Waterloo is part of a longstanding pattern of American hospitality toward strangers, including Muslims, even though— and this is the paradox we will have to wrestle with—America has always been suspicious of foreign cultures and has been entrapped in a seemingly never-ending conflict with the Islamic world.

For the longest time, I thought that if Americans and Muslims could dispel many of the prejudices they held about each other, the United States and Muslim-majority nations would have a better chance at achieving better relations and even forge meaningful partnerships and alliances. Assuming that Iowans could have swarthy complexions, the Muslim woman at Waterloo could have passed for a native Iowan. She also could have been another Rima Fakih, the twenty-four-year-old Shiite Muslim from Lebanon who won the title of Miss USA a few days later. She certainly did not look like the fist-waving, flag-burning, shrouded anti-American protesters one often comes across in mainstream publications.

I also witnessed America at its finest when my five-year-old son was diagnosed with acute myeloid leukemia in February 2004. The day I had to take my son to the hospital, my wife, who was home with our toddler and a four-year-old boy, looked frantically for someone to stay with the children while she rushed to join us. A neighbor willingly did while relatives drove up from the state of New Hampshire to stay longer. Then our neighbors (many of whom were born and raised in the area) set up a system of support and prayers that worked for months. Day after day, food was delivered to our house, sometimes by people we knew, others by people we had never met. Some started taking our children while we had to attend to urgent medical matters, even offering to spend the night at our house and watch over them. My son's name was added to prayer lists in our neighborhood churches. Friends from afar wrote or called us to tell us about prayers conducted in New Mexico by Dakota, Apache, and other Native American healers; in California by Buddhists; in New Hampshire by Baptists; in New York, Washington, D.C., and other places by different religions. Our Jewish friends prayed for our son, inundated us with love and care, and a family that lived in the hospital area opened their home to me anytime I wanted to take a break from the hospital for a good meal or a nap. Atheists from all religious backgrounds offered sincere support. My employer, the University of New England, made it easy for me to stay with my son during his seven-month ordeal at the hospital.

During this time, my son's school nurse came to visit him and started a bone marrow drive for him and another child whose acute lymphoblastic leukemia had relapsed. Posters with photographs of the two children were made and distributed in local supermarkets and stores. The event was covered in local papers. My son's teacher came to visit several times in the hospital and our house, teaching and supporting him along the way. The school principal came to check on him when his life was in serious danger at the intensive care unit. Meanwhile, about 380 people volunteered to give their bone marrow on a Saturday, stretching the logistical limits of the operation. Help and love kept pouring in. Food and gifts never ceased appearing at our home's doorstep.

In the midst of this overwhelming generosity, I remember getting a phone call from a Moroccan engineer in Massachusetts to talk about academic matters. Upon hearing about my son's illness, he suggested that I come to his area because it has an extensive Muslim community that includes two physicians. When I told him about the support we were getting he seemed incredulous, as if he didn't expect that to happen in the United States, or as if Muslims could do better. His was the only such opinion I heard. The typical response of most of my family and Muslim friends was that I was lucky to be in the United States where medical care is highly advanced.

My son needed huge supplies of blood and platelet transfusions to offset the effects of the chemotherapy that destroys good and bad cells in his bone marrow. The blood he received, all donated by volunteers, was carefully screened and properly radiated. Without these massive blood transfusions, administered over a period of seven months, my son would not have survived. Moreover, as we were wondering about a bone marrow match for our son—his two siblings, mother, and I didn't match—we learned that most donors were of European descent, which might have limited the options for our mixed-ancestry son. In short, in the most vital profession to human life, one that best mirrors the virtues of mercy and love enshrined in every religion, Americans (as well as most Western nations) are so far ahead of Muslims that the two might as well be living in two different planets.

Muslims were once leaders, as had been other civilizations, like the Chinese, but have now fallen so badly behind that they are totally engrossed in socially and politically ruinous struggles for power and authority, arguing over arcane and meaningless religious details, while many nations are forging ahead into the future and adopting new ways of thinking. The United Nations–sponsored and Arab-authored Arab Human Development reports of the first decade of our century leave no doubt about the extent to which Muslim and Arab cultures have deteriorated. When China published a list of the world's five hundred best universities in 2003, it didn't list a single Arab university.[13]

It is not that contemporary Arabs or Muslims don't have much to contribute to world civilization or to American culture; they certainly do and their impact, as this book will show later, is lasting and profound. But they do so within the open systems of the West and America, not through the stifling bureaucracies of the Arab and Muslim worlds. This is why the Arab and Muslim brain drain is high. It is not for no reason that a poll taken in 2009 revealed what had been intuitively obvious to many of us who left our native countries: Muslims, particularly immigrants or their descendants, are more likely to thrive in the United States than in any other part of the world, including, of course, the Muslim-majority societies they left behind.[14]

My son's sickness and my frantic attempts to find answers led me to the Web page of a Lebanese physician and accomplished researcher in the field of childhood leukemia, particularly my son's kind, practicing in St. Jude Children's Research Hospital—America's, and probably the world's, most famous hospital specializing in catastrophic illnesses in children. I emailed him and, from Lebanon, he wrote back offering support. Within days we were back in touch and he became an invaluable advisor as I thought about and agonized over my son's condition. I had known that my son's primary physician, a nationally known authority in the field of childhood leukemia, one of the most humane and intelligent physicians anyone is ever likely to find, had practiced in St. Jude before he came to Maine; but now I found out that he had been the Lebanese doctor's mentor as well. Then, as I tried to find out about St. Jude hospital, I realized that it had been founded by an Arab American who had prayed to St. Jude (the patron saint of lost causes) when he was down on his luck and vowed that he'd do a good deed if his fortunes improved. (To be sure, Danny Thomas, like others that will be mentioned in the book, was Christian, not Muslim, but, as I alluded to in the preface, by virtue of his parents' native language and background, as well as by the Islamic culture that has historically embraced non-Muslims, he also, unwittingly perhaps, stands for Islam in the United States. Most Arab American organizations in the United States today, although often led by men and women from Christian backgrounds, resist anti-Arab discrimination and Islamophobia because they consider the culture of Islam as an inextricable part of the Arab heritage.)

The fortunes of Danny Thomas, né Muzyad Yahkoub in Deerfield, Michigan, did improve as he soon became a TV celebrity highly respected for his integrity (he protected two black-listed writers who wrote for his show in the 1950s from anticommunist zealots). When he reached his dream, as many still do in the United States (despite the ongoing onslaught on the edifice of the US economy and the growing despair of millions of hard-working, unemployed Americans), Thomas remembered his vow and, with the help of an Arab American philanthropic organization, raised funds to start building the hospital in Memphis, Tennessee. America had opened its door to Arabs, who now paid back by helping the most vulnerable members of the human family. Not only that, but Danny Thomas also vowed that his hospital would accept rich and poor, insured and uninsured alike, and make the cutting-edge research conducted in the hospital instantly available to the international medical community.

The grandeur of such vision, the wherewithal to do it, the support and legal systems to make it possible, and the social encouragement for such a monumental endeavor could only have happened in America. In Arab and Muslim countries, these are mammoth state projects at best. I very much doubt that Danny Thomas would have ever been able to fulfill his vow had he been in a Muslim or Arab country. For his exceptional humanitarian and artistic work, Danny Thomas was nominated for a Nobel Peace Prize, awarded the Congressional Medal of Honor, and received numerous prestigious prizes and decorations.[15] On the night of September 18, 2004, eight days after my son was discharged from the hospital, his daughter, Marlo Thomas, an actress in her own right and spokesperson for St. Jude Hospital, accepted the Bob Hope Humanitarian Award on behalf of her father, who had passed away in 1991.

Danny Thomas was not, by any means, the only Arab or Muslim who had an impact on American and, indeed, global medicine through the opportunities American society makes available to all sorts of immigrants and their children. Decades before Thomas built his hospital, Dr. Michael Shadid, an Arab immigrant who worked hard peddling jewelry before obtaining a medical degree, grew so dismayed by the plight of poor farmers in Oklahoma and the way they were fleeced by greedy and criminally incompetent physicians that he fought hard to establish the first cooperative hospital in the country at Elk City. For only twenty-five dollars, a family of four could get basic medical care, not including hospitalization and medicine, for a whole year. The progressive Arab also served as president of the Cooperative Health Federation of America (1947–1949), which he helped found.[16]

A far better-known American physician of Arab descent is Dr. Michael E. DeBakey, "the greatest surgeon ever," as the *Journal of the American Medical Association* concluded in 2005. Dr. DeBakey lived and worked in the United States, where he revolutionized heart surgery procedures and advised American and world leaders until his death at the age of ninety-nine in 2008. Born in the state of Louisiana in 1908 to Christian Lebanese parents (his mother taught him to sew, crochet, and knit while his father ran a pharmacy that attracted local physicians), he probably would not have achieved so much had his parents not fled religious persecution in their native Arab land. Dr. DeBakey was honored with a Presidential Medal of Freedom in 1969, a National Medal of Science in 1987, and a Congressional Gold Medal in 2008, the year he passed away.[17]

Six years earlier, and not long after the terrorist attacks of 9/11, when the image of Muslims, Arabs, and North Africans in general was severely undermined, President George W. Bush appointed the Algerian-born and educated Dr. Elias A. Zerhouni to run the National Institutes of Health, America's most powerful medical research agency, overseeing more than seventeen thousand employees across a complex of twenty-seven institutes and centers and a twenty-four-billion-dollar budget. Like many immigrants, Dr. Zerhouni would not have guessed that when he arrived in to the United States as an immigrant with $369 in his pocket in 1975, he would rise to such a status. America treated him well and he was grateful, he told an interviewer after one year at the job.[18]

The world of music, too, has been seriously impacted by Arabs or Muslims. When the video clip of Danny Thomas's work shown on the big theater screen in 2004, it was narrated by the Detroit-born Arab American radio personality Casey Kasem, known as "King of the Countdowns," for originating the era-defining radio "American Top 40" and changing the way people listened to pop music. Few Americans have heard of Ahmet Ertegün, but this Muslim Turkish American (born Ahmet Munir in Turkey in 1923) who passed away at age eighty-three in 2006, was described by the *Independent*, a British newspaper, as "the most important figure in the record industry of the 20th century" for having founded Atlantic Records, the independent label that signed up some of the best musicians of our time, ranging from Ray Charles to the Rolling Stones. A few months after Ertegün died, PBS aired a documentary about his life and work as part of its "American Masters" series. The title was: "Atlantic Records: The House That Ahmet Built." (Ahmet's father, Munir Ertegün, had made an equally powerful impression on the United States. He had served his country, Turkey, with so much aplomb as ambassador that when he died President Harry Truman sent his body to Turkey on the USS *Missouri* and American naval officers marched with Turkish soldiers in honor of the dead Muslim man.) The cases of Danny Thomas, Dr. Michael Shadid, Dr. Michael DeBakey, Dr. Elias Zerhouni, Ahmet Ertegün, and Casey Kasem show that medicine and pop music would not have been what they are today without Arabs and Muslims working freely in the United States.[19] The same applies to Muslim women. While many Muslims are bemoaning the lax moral standards of the West, and those of the United States in particular, no country has been more liberating to ambitious, entrepreneurial Muslim women that the United States. Two articles published in the *New York Times* after Christmas 2010 captured this reality most poignantly. The first one, titled "Necessity Pushes Pakistani Women Into Jobs and Peril," is an account of the banishment and beatings inflicted on Pakistani women who are forced by economic necessity to seek work in places like McDonald's or in supermarkets. The sexual codes in Pakistan appear to be so distorted that merely smiling at a customer in the line of duty invites life-threatening episodes of harassment. It is, therefore, logical that Pakistan and other Muslim-majority nations are the worst-ranking nations in the 2010 Global Gender Gap Report. Two days after this dispiriting report was published, the *Times* published a report about the great level of success achieved by Muslim women in the United States. Titled "Muslim Women Gain Higher Profile in U.S.," the article shows how America's culture of freedom has allowed pious Muslim women to lead major Islamic organizations, publish magazines, and lead fulfilling lives despite social discrimination, and reach earning equity with Muslim men.[20]

Even when Muslims get in trouble with the law and are caught in the web of arrests following 9/11, their belief in the possibilities of America remained undimmed. In October 2004, newspapers published the account of a twenty-six-year-old Moroccan terrorism suspect who had once been accused of being part of a "sleeper operational combat cell" based in Detroit. The Moroccan immigrant, detained on September 17, 2001 and released on October 12, 2004, described a harrowing jail experience that could send shivers across the Muslim world: but the Muslim man was steadfastly defended by his lawyers, and the judge threw out his conviction after the government failed to produce incriminating evidence. The Moroccan was still facing document fraud charges and the prospect of deportation;

yet, despite his suffering, he preferred staying in the United States to going back to his native country. "I want to live the dream—the American dream," he declared. "That's what I came here for, what everybody has come and will come to America for," he said after his release.[21]

Muslim detainees held at Guantánamo Bay prison were subjected to a far worse fate, as most never got to see their day in court. But as improbable as it may seem, even this universally condemned facility managed to reflect some of the American values that millions of Muslims and Arabs find liberating. Prayer times were kept, *halal* food was served, and health care services were provided. Many people may have been perplexed when, in 2010, they learned that six Algerian detainees at Guantánamo preferred to stay in that prison facility rather than being back in their home country.[22] There are few stronger testaments to the hope and promise of America.

And what is true for Arabs is also true for other nationalities and ethnicities. In 2004, President Bush nominated the son of migrant workers from Mexico, forty-nine-year-old Alberto R. Gonzales, to the post of Attorney General, the nation's top law enforcement officer, and a Cuban-born corporate executive, Carlos M. Gutierrez, to be Secretary of Commerce.[23] That same year, Arnold Schwarzenegger, an Austrian man who started out as body builder, was governor of California, the land of fabled dreams, the most populous state in the union, and, if considered a nation apart, one of the world's top economies. Another foreign-born woman (from British Columbia, Canada), Jennifer M. Granholm, was governor of Michigan, then the nation's leading automobile manufacturer. The two governors were so admired that people were beginning to talk about a constitutional amendment to lift the restrictions on foreign-born citizens becoming president of the United States. If these two politicians had run for president in 2004, either one of them could have been a solid contender in the election.

Although, as I shall show at more length in the last chapter, the United States seems to be reneging on its revolutionary and egalitarian principles, and public good has been hijacked by voracious private interests, opportunities also abound for white Americans born into the lower rungs of society. The two contenders for the American presidency in 2004 were children of privilege, both graduates of the elite university of Yale, but that doesn't mean those with lesser pedigrees don't reach up higher in the realm of government. Not long after Bush had nominated Alberto R. Gonzales and Carlos M. Gutierrez for top government positions, the Republican president chose forty-nine-year-old Bernard B. Kerik—a man who, as a toddler, was abandoned by his prostitute mother (who was probably later killed by her pimp), dropped out of high school, declared bankruptcy, ran a jail in New Jersey, supervised the security of Saudi royal hospitals, worked as an undercover detective, and eventually rose to New York City police commissioner, a post he held during the terrorist attacks of 9/11—to run the newly created Department of Homeland Security.[24] Kerik eventually withdrew his nomination after it turned out that he had hired an illegal immigrant nanny and engaged in other illegal activities. After a decade of legal wrangling, he was finally sent to prison in 2010.[25] Still, the fact that he had been chosen for this powerful post attests to the opportunities available to average Americans.

My own state of Maine never ceases to amaze me with its can-do spirit, faith in hard work and opportunity, and an inborn resistance to national trends manufactured by the media. During the time I have lived in that state, an independent man was elected governor, two women have served as Republican senators, and some of the most progressive men and women in the country were elected to Congress and other local offices. In 2010, voters gave a chance to a Republican candidate for governor in a three-way race to hold office. Without much coaching in the language of diplomacy, Paul LePage quickly got in trouble. But what interests me most in Governor LePage's story is not his politics but that he was able to reach the pinnacle of power in a state where he started out disadvantaged and homeless. When he was eleven, he ran away from his dysfunctional home and lived on the streets shining shoes before he was adopted and given a chance to enroll in Husson College despite his poor English. He worked hard, excelled in his studies, did well in business and politics, and is, at the time of this writing, governor. This is yet another example of the unique possibilities the United States offers its citizens.

Despite America's checkered history, no nation has brought as many diverse people together and allowed all—irrespective of race, color, and background—to do as well. The United States is, as Walt Whitman put it, a "race of races." Most Old World nations appeal to an older identity, using it to exclude minorities from well-guarded spheres of influence. How long, if ever, would it take China to appoint a German-born Henry Kissinger or African American Colin

Powell and Condoleeza Rice for Minister of Foreign Affairs? Which European country can entrust its most powerful medical research agency and a twenty-four-billion-dollar budget to an Algerian immigrant? In which nation could a body builder immigrant who still speaks with a heavy accent become, in the course of a few decades, one of the most powerful politicians in his host country? And is there any country that would elect Barack Hussein Obama as president? Obama would have never been elected in Kenya, the land of his father, or any African nation, for that matter. People from an immigrant background in rich Arab or Muslim nations are tremendously lucky if they are given citizenships, but they simply have no chance of ever assuming high political positions. The African and Muslim-majority countries that complain loudly about European xenophobia are far more xenophobic in their treatment of foreigners, even those who have spent a lifetime, or even two generations or more, in their midst. Europe is fairer to its nonnative residents, but it is not remotely close to the United States in the opportunities it provides to hard-working immigrants.

When my son was being treated at the Barbara Bush Children's Hospital, a unit of the Maine Medical Center in Portland, Maine, hospital officials decided to design a new dress to accommodate Muslim women patients who feel exposed by wearing the traditional medical garb called "Johnny" or "Johnnie." A few people wrote to the hospital complaining about reverse discrimination and preferential treatment upon hearing about this new policy, but the hospital stuck with its decision, even though the Muslim population (mostly Somalis) it was serving was minuscule.[26] In Minneapolis, Minnesota, too, the Hennepin County Medical Center is acting heroically to accommodate its Somali Muslim patients. (It might be instructive to compare these examples of tolerance to France, where it is much harder for Muslims to express their religious affiliation in public institutions.)

When Morocco's ambassador in Washington, D.C. visited us with his family, a delegation from the hospital welcomed him and offered him and my son autographed copies of Mrs. Barbara Bush's reflections on life after the White House. (Her daughter, Pauline Robinson, or Robin, had suffered a tragic fate. She was born in 1949 and passed away of leukemia in 1953, when she was still three years old. Her death had a major impact on her parents and older brother, George W. Bush, the forty-third president of the United States.[27]) Later, my son and I, together with other patients, families, and staff, celebrated

Barbara Bush's birthday in the sunlit and welcoming atrium, while she was away in Washington attending the funeral procession of former President Ronald Reagan. When she came to the hospital, read stories to children, and gave out more signed copies of children's books later that year, my son couldn't attend because he was too sick to leave his room. Five years later, the new president of my university invited him and his siblings to watch a private showing of a new *Star Trek* film with the Bushes at an IMAX theater in Saco, Maine. My son took his autographed book with him, and, right in the movie theater, when the show was over, Mrs. Bush inscribed his name on it, as she and her husband, the former president, expressed the best of grandparental affections to him and his siblings.

This is an example of the America I have experienced, one that is not well conveyed to the Muslim world. To be sure, relations have improved since the election of Obama in late 2008, but major hurdles remain in the still elusive dialogue between non-Muslim Americans and Muslims in general. When President Obama's envoy to the Muslim world met with a well-educated Pakistani journalist in August 2009, the journalist didn't mince his words: "You should know that we all hate Americans," the journalist told his interlocutor, because Americans simply don't care about the welfare of Muslims. By the end of 2010, the world's Muslims' fervor for Obama had cooled down substantially. Few believed in his promise.

We can't, however, give up on change. Muslims need to have a more nuanced knowledge of America and not simply see the nation that launched the first republican government in modern history, enshrined deep-seated notions of freedom, and gave opportunities to many Muslims and members of other ethnic or immigrant groups to flourish as a rapacious colonial empire, bent of depriving nations of their God-given resources and turning Muslims into the wretched of the Earth. Muslim and Arab Americans wouldn't do as well as they have if the United States of America were not an open society that offers opportunities to members of all faiths and ethnicities. Even when the US government is engaged in war with Muslim states, the fate of most Muslims, or people of Muslim descent, remains mostly unaffected.

A genuine dialogue between the United States and non-American Muslims around the globe could not start without, as President Obama suggested in his historic address to the Muslim world in Cairo, some recognition of each nation's failings. There is no shortage of books praising Islam as a great civilization, or dismissing it as a barbaric relic, but such apologies or denunciations do not help us grasp the complex and changing history of the United States and the Islamic world, including its Arab component. We need, in other words, to learn from the past.

I know for a fact that Muslims and Americans can engage in meaningful discussions that can lead to progress, if such discussions are anchored in some knowledge of history. I witnessed such debates in Rabat, Morocco's capital, in 2005, after I had given a lecture to a packed hall of Moroccan and American students, as well as a couple of officers from the US embassy, on the meaning of American freedom. At that time, the US government was trying hard to reach Muslims, but Muslim skepticism and fear were aggravated by US military actions in the region and by the aspersions cast on their religion in the media. Still, the topic of freedom generated such a lively debate that it planted the idea for this project in my consciousness.

As I did with the topic of freedom in Rabat, I am using this book to survey American–Muslim relations within the old clash of religions before we ask ourselves—Muslims and non-Muslims alike—whether our beliefs and prejudices still make sense today. I wouldn't be surprised if my readers—American and Muslim, Israeli and Palestinian, Jew and Arab, or just simply religious and secular—found themselves uncomfortable at different points in the narrative. No nation, religion, or ethnicity gets a free pass, not because I want to be provocative, but because I am at a point in my life when, both intellectually and, even more importantly, *emotionally*, such rigid tribal divisions mean very little to me. The blind passions they engender are plunging our already fractured world into a deepening abyss. If gun lobbyists in the United States often claim that people—not guns—kill, then we must make sure that people carrying guns are not ideologically predisposed to shoot. I do respect the intensity of religion or nationalist convictions, but I also hope that such sentiments do not prevent us from engaging in serious conversations about our common future.

I have my own biases, of course, but the goal is to try to rise above them through self-reflection and by taking measure of one's place in the cosmic scheme of things. I know I keep readjusting my lenses as time goes by. As someone who objects to the domination of one cultural entity over another, I started out being suspicious of the Enlightenment because I thought it was yet another example of how Europeans manage to impose their views on the rest of the world. Yet now, more than a decade later, I find myself firmly in its most radical grip. Good, humane ideas, I have concluded, have no nationality. Cultures borrow from each other and give new life to old ideas. That's how human history moves. Would Christianity and Islam exist if there had been no Judaism in the first place? To me, both Christianity and Islam seem to be variations on the Jewish theme. But single-minded believers don't see it this way. There can only be one god, not many. Open-endedness, or the ability to say yes and no, or, even more *a propos*, to say yes and yes, is a threat to such monotheistic convictions. And so people are sentenced to clash.

Chapter 1

America's View of Islam

When President Obama stood in front of the Turkish parliament in Ankara he said to much applause that the "United States is not, and will never be, at war with Islam." When he spoke from Cairo in 2009, Jakarta in 2010, and from Washington, D.C. on the night of May 1, 2011, to announce the death of Osama bin Laden in Pakistan, he emphasized the point, as if to make sure that Muslims understand that the United States has no ill will toward their faith. Technically, this is true, since the US government doesn't do business or go to war with religions; but to the extent that any government is shaped by the beliefs and mores of the society it serves, Obama's statement dodges an uncomfortable truth about American–Muslim relations. As the heir to a long, albeit reformed, European Christian tradition, Protestant America has consistently held a negative image of Islam and Muslims.

Obama may have been echoing an eighteenth-century clause in a US treaty with Muslim Tripoli, one of the so-called Barbary States, ratified in 1797. Article 11 of that treaty unambiguously denies that the United States was at war with Islam. It said: "As the government of the United States of America is not in any sense founded on the Christian Religion—as it has in itself no character of enmity against the laws, religion, or tranquility of Musselmen—and as the said States never have entered into any war or act of hostility against any Mehomitan nation, it is declared by the parties that no pretext arising from religious opinions shall ever produce an interruption of the harmony existing between the two countries."[1] But such language, even if it reflected the views of progressive Americans at the time, didn't change the fact that Protestant Americans believed that Islam

23

was a fraudulent religion that needed to be uprooted from the Middle East, or that many of them sought to restore Jews to the Holy Land in preparation of the Second Coming. The United States may not be at war with Muslims because of their faith, but America has always been in conflict with Islam. This is one aspect of the American past that I understand Obama was asking us to change. Unmodified or unchallenged, certain tenets of the Christian faith in the United States will continue to stoke the fires of discord.

When Muslim terrorists attacked the United States on September 11, 2001, Americans, once again, awoke to a perplexing religion, one that seemed atavistic and violent, as if a mindset buried in the depths of history simply erupted back to shatter everything modern civilization was supposed to be. Nonpolitically correct public figures didn't hesitate in calling Islam backward and violent; they even accused the prophet of Islam of being a terrorist or a sick man. The evangelical leader, Rod Parsley, once a spiritual advisor to Obama's Republican challenger for the US presidency, John McCain, and author of *Silent No More* (2005), called Islam the "anti-Christ religion" and added: "The fact is that America was founded, in part, with the intention of seeing this false religion destroyed, and I believe September 11, 2001, was a generational call to arms that we can no longer ignore." The Rev. John Hagee, another supporter of McCain, and a founder Christians United for Israel (CUFI), saw the United States engaged in a religious war with Islam. Franklin Graham is famous for saying that Islam is "a very evil and wicked religion," Pat Robertson for describing Mohammed as "an absolute wild-eyed fanatic . . . a robber . . . a brigand . . . a killer," and Jerry Falwell for calling the Muslim prophet a "terrorist" on national television.[2] In the summer of 2010, when the plan to build an Islamic community center near Ground Zero in Manhattan was the main controversy of the day, Terry Jones, a pastor at a nondenominational church in Gainseville, Florida, declared his intention to host an "International Burn the Quran Day" on the upcoming anniversary of 9/11. Speaking to a CNN anchor, he said: "We believe that Islam is of the devil, that it's causing billions of people to go to hell, it is a deceptive religion, it is a violent religion and that is proven many, many times."[3] Only when he was opposed by an international uproar, including by members of the US government and military, did he relent and postpone his plan, which he quietly carried out (in a smaller but still controversial ceremony) the following year.

Secular liberals object vigorously to such supremacist attitudes, while most American churches, as well as a number of progressive evangelicals, denounce such belligerence in the name of the Lord as, well, ungodly. Well-intentioned scholars, journalists, and politicians, including the president of the United States, continue to do everything they can to separate Islam, the religion of about one-and-a-half billion of the world's population, spread out across the globe, from the despicable actions of a few terrorists. Policy initiatives have been designed to reach Muslim hearts and minds, and calls are often made for understanding Islam and engaging in a better dialogue with its adherents. The US government has consistently made clear that its wars and skirmishes in Afghanistan, Iraq, Somalia, and Pakistan have nothing to do with Islam; they were, or still are, merely operations for self-defense and necessary undertakings in the war on terror.

Despite America's willingness to extend its hand to Muslims, as Obama said in his inaugural address in January 2009, American values remain quite unfamiliar to non-American Muslims. Americans and Muslims hear a lot about each other, but neither side has gone into a deeper comprehension of the causes that divide the two cultures. If the Americans seeking genuine dialogue with Muslims had done so, they would have found out that the anti-Islamic utterances of prominent evangelicals and conservatives after 9/11 are part of a pattern that goes back to the first European pilgrims. America, whether in its colonial phase or in its postrevolutionary one, has always seen Islam as a religion fostering tyranny. Islam may have had good things to offer every now and then, but American civilization, in both its Christian and secular formulations, was built in opposition to Islam. There is still no reason to believe that this is not the case today.

The European discovery of the American continent itself was conceived as a step in the ultimate defeat of Islam. Christian Europe had been in a state of conflict and war with Islam for so long that such animosities were part of the baggage European sailors brought with them to America in 1492. That year, Granada, the last bastion of Islam in Spain, fell to Spain's Catholic forces, an event that was heralded as the first step in the defeat of Islam and its expulsion from the Christian lands lost to that faith. Christopher Columbus, for example, believed that he was predestined to lead a "fifth Crusade" and reconquer Jerusalem,[4] thereby setting the tone for centuries to come, even though the most ardent pursuers of this goal would be

Protestant, not Catholic. One may think that we have come a long
way since the days of the Crusades and the Spanish reconquests of
the Middle Ages, but such Christian passions and prejudices have a
way of being hardwired into a cultural tradition.

Because I am aware of the long history dividing the United States
and the world of Islam, I find traces of this old conflict in the most
mundane of places. For instance, in early January 2009, when the
main news of the day was Israel's invasion of the Gaza strip, I happened to be sitting in a small sauna in Maine next to a veteran of the
Gulf War who was intent on losing weight through sweating. Next
to him sat a man who sounded as if he were a veteran from an earlier
war, since both men spoke quite knowledgeably about the military.
At one point, I said that war in the Middle East doesn't seem to end.
The first man agreed, "Oh, no, it will never end. It's in the Bible."
Then, he added, "Maybe what's his name—Obama—can help."

These men, I assumed, were not liberals or Democrats. They were
the sort of folks many secular liberals would contemptuously dismiss
as dangerously biased, unenlightened people who probably don't like
Muslims and are not fond of the first African American president of
the United States, a man who had been repeatedly labeled Muslim
by his detractors during the presidential campaign the previous year.
Be that as it may, though, the warriors in the sauna were expressing
a very American sentiment, including, perhaps, and if one is willing
to be indulgent, that a multicultural president with vaguely Islamic
connections, and one who is not part of America's colonial mindset,
might find a way to forge better relations with America's historic
religious enemy. President Obama's election in 2008 gave Americans and Muslims an unprecedented opportunity to connect, one that
is worth our time to build on.

In any case, the men's reliance on the Bible to make sense of the
Middle East has a long pedigree in American thought and, in fact,
explains much about the current conflict in the Middle East. The central lands of Islam have always repulsed and fascinated Americans
simultaneously. Early preachers were thankful that America was
as far as could possibly be from the Middle East and North Africa.
Cotton Mather, the clergyman from Massachusetts, relished the fact
that he was in a country "afar off, in a Land, which never had (that
I ever heard of) one Mahometan breathing in it." Mather's vitriol
for Islam was constant. He wrote that smallpox was brought into
Europe "on the Wings of those *Arabian* Locusts, that in the *Saracen*

Conquests did *spread over the Face of the Earth.*" In 1696, he pronounced that *"The Day is at Hand*, when the *Turkish Empire*, instead
of being any longer a *Wo* to *Chistendome*, shall it self become a *Part
of Christendome.*"⁵ Mather may even have set the tone for the current evangelical dismissal of Mohammed as a violent man by calling
him—in a 1721 treatise titled *The Christian Philosopher*—a "thick-
skull'd Prophet."⁶ Others saw the Muslim prophet as an impostor,
immoral hedonist, or an epileptic. Roger Williams, the Baptist leader
of Rhode Island who found Roman Catholicism, Quakerism, and
Islam to be equally deceitful, called him "that stupendious Cheater."⁷
Compared to the bright light of Christianity, with its gentle mores,
Islam represented sensuality, deceit, despotism, and ignorance,
among other bad traits.

Early captivity narratives—that is, the narratives of men (and
women) presumably captured by North African Muslim pirates
waging *jihad* against Christian vessels, perhaps like the renegade
Somalis have been doing recently—were used as occasions to preach
against the depredations of Islam or those of sultans like the infamous Moroccan Moulay Ismail, whose notorious cruelty, according
to one account by the English captive Francis Brooks, was due to
religious and racial defects. (Moulay Ismail's mother was black.)
The Moroccan sultan loomed so large in New England's imagination
that Cotton Mather addressed him directly in *The Goodness of God.*
And because the specter of blacks enslaving whites was possible (at
least in other parts of the world), the Virginia House of Burgesses
outlawed the possibility of "Negros, Mulattos, or Indians" owning
white Christians as slaves, although such a right was, intriguingly,
extended to "Christians, or Jews, Moors, Mahometans, or other
infidels."⁸

Such sentiments were more or less shared by members of the
Revolutionary generation. Baron de Montesquieu's *The Spirit of the
Laws* (1748), a book condemning Oriental and Islamic despotism,
was probably more widely read than even the work of the English
philosopher John Locke, whose work had an indelible imprint on
the Declaration of Independence and the American Revolution.⁹ In
Common Sense, Tom Paine compared the abuses of the British mon-
archy to those of the papacy and Islam; John Adams compared his
rival Jefferson to Mohammed, whose followers repeat the Muslim
declaration of faith, adapted to American politics, "There is but one
Goddess of Liberty, and Common Sense is her Prophet."¹⁰ As the

historian Robert J. Allison noted in *The Crescent Obscured*, Islam was treated by all political factions as the antithesis of liberty. There was bipartisan agreement, to use today's political lingo, that Islam encouraged a despotism that inevitably leads to economic and cultural ruin. Many Americans, when they surveyed the history of North Africa, attributed the region's former glory to the Carthaginians and Romans. America's Christian prejudices were manifest in the iconography of the Revolution itself. The story of Moses leading Israelites to the Promised Land was the main theme of early American symbolism. The journey included, of course, the conquest of Canaanites, as Timothy Dwight titled his epic celebration of American independence in 1777, and which he dedicated to George Washington, "The Saviour of his Country, the Supporter of Freedom, and the Benefactor of Mankind."[11] Joel Barlow's poem *The Vision of Columbus* (1787) even compares Columbus's voyage to the New World to the Israelites' journey to the Promised Land:

As the great Seer, whose animating rod
Taught Israel's sons the wonder-working God,
Who led, thro' dreary wastes, the murmuring band
To the fair confines of the promised land,
Oppress'd with years, from Pisgah's beauteous height,
O'er boundless regions cast the captured sight;
The joys of unborn nations warm'd his breast,
Repaid his toils and sooth'd his soil to rest.[12]

One could already tell that America's new blend of revolutionary, democratic Protestantism was to have a major impact on the Middle East and Islam.

Indeed, the new nation's first war was with Muslim corsairs from the Barbary states (particularly Algiers and Tripoli) consolidated American patriotism. Although Barbary pirates not infrequently engaged in lawful business activity, they allowed Americans to intensify the contrast between their free, bright, civilized republic and the dark, barbaric, and despotic culture of Islam. A few were aware of the long Christian–Muslim wars, but the Barbary States were still a "nest of banditti," as John Adams and George Washington described them.[13] John Jay threatened New Yorkers in 1787 that if they didn't ratify the new Constitution, "Algerians could be on the American coast and enslave its citizens who have not a single sloop of war."[14] A 1799 report described Algerians as lazy, undisciplined, weak, and praying "away their lives under the shrines of departed saints."[15] Several scholars and commentators recalled this episode in American history after 9/11. The conservative British historian Paul Johnson even called for colonialism as a solution to the problem of terrorism.[16]

Yet, whether in 1801 or 2001, the United States had no problem prevailing militarily over what some today might call Muslim "rogue states." In fact, even as suspicious-looking aliens were being deported from Virginia, the state's legislature passed an act in 1786, written by Thomas Jefferson, to protect the religious freedom of Muslims. Jefferson also pushed hard for a navy that finally defeated Tripoli and ended its harassment of US vessels in the Mediterranean, a feat commemorated in the "Marines' Hymn"—"to the shores of Tripoli"—and in the curved Mameluke swords carried by corps officers to this day. Even the US national anthem traces its lineage to the war on Muslim corsairs. In a little-known 1805 poem in honor of Stephen Decatur that would become the prototype for the national anthem, Francis Scott Key, author of "The Star-Spangled Banner," celebrated the American heroes of the Barbary wars in a language that foreshadowed the present conflict in the Middle East:

In the conflict resistless each toil they endured,
'Till their foes fled dismayed from the war's desolation;
And pale beamed the crescent, its splendor obscured
By the light of the star-spangled flag of our nation.
Where each radiant star gleamed a meteor of war,
And the turbaned heads bowed to its terrible glare,
Now mixed with the olive the laurel shall wave,
And form a bright wreath for the brow of the brave.[17]

Islam was simply un-American, and that perception remains very strong today. When the African American Muslim Keith Ellison was elected in Minneapolis to Congress in 2006, some major media personalities were taken aback at the prospect of a Muslim taking an oath of office on the Qur'an. The influential talk-show host Glenn Beck asked Ellison point blank to prove that he was not an enemy of the United States. It was a remarkable exchange, full of historical ironies. The Mormon Beck must surely have been aware that when Mormonism was born the new faith was viewed with equal suspicion by the US Congress, as well as by the American people who actually, in some instances, declared war on the Mormons.

In fact, Mormonism was so un-American throughout the nineteenth century that it was initially seen as a ploy by Muslims to infiltrate America. The Mormon trek across the country became a *hijra*; the Mormons' many wives, *houris*; Utah, the Holy Land; Salt Lake City, a new Mecca. This is not to forget that Joseph Smith, Jr. was called "the Yankee Mahomet," or "the American Mahomet," and his book, the Book of Mormon, a new Qur'an. Brigham Young, who took over after Smith's death, was also called "the New World Mohammed" and "the Mahomet of Salt Lake." And so it went, with the issue of polygamy giving further ammunition to the new religion's detractors. Novels, plays, and poems depicted a world of harems and seraglios. In her book, *The Women of Mormonism* (1882), Frances Willard, the president of the Woman's Christian Temperance Union, saw Utah as nothing less than Turkey in America:

> Turkey is in our midst. Modern Mohammedanism has its Mecca at Salt Lake, where Prophet Heber C. Kimball speaks of his wives as "cows." Clearly the Koran was Joseph Smith's model, so closely followed as to exclude even the poor pretension of originality in his foul "revelation."[18]

Although Americans expressed fear of Islam at home, they didn't hesitate to meet Muslims abroad. The Revolution had taught Americans to think of themselves as world leaders. "Every free citizen of the American Empire," pronounced the poet Joel Barlow on his nation's eleventh Fourth of July, "ought now to consider himself as the legislator of half mankind."[19] And so, no sooner had the dust settled on the Revolution than Americans directed their sight on the lands of Islam. Empowered by their new status among nations, they sailed out confidently, if a bit naively and arrogantly, to reshape the Holy Land in their image. Here's the Presbyterian missionary Samuel Worcester's address, in 1805, to American missionaries on their way to the Middle East:

> Go, and from the heights of Calvary and of Zion proclaim to the long last tribes of Israel, to the followers of the Pseudo-prophet, to the bewildered people of different lands, tongues, and religions, the fountains there opened, for the cleansing of all nations—the banner there displayed, for the gathering of all people.[20]

Worcester was expressing the long-held Puritan view that there was too much religious diversity in the Holy Land, or what, in

1671, a patriarch of the Maronite Church had called a "chaos of confessions."[21] The Ottomans had granted various religious communities, or "millets," the right to maintain their autonomy within the framework of their Sunni state religion. Sunni Muslims, Shiites, Druze, Maronite Christians, Catholics, and Jews all lived together in the Holy Land and coexisted rather peacefully, particularly in neighboring regions such as Mount Lebanon. Here communities borrowed from one another freely; they wore the same dress and ate the same food. American Protestants were utterly unprepared for the clash of cultures that awaited them. Like Wahhabis today with non-Wahhabi Muslims or non-Muslims, American Protestant missionaries had no idea how to coexist with other varieties of Christianity, let alone non-Christians. They simply didn't know how to fit into the rich textual fabric of Middle Eastern reality.[22]

American missionaries were, however, received cordially and were shown, as tradition dictated, a good amount of hospitality. But, like Jonas King, a man who studied Arabic in France with the well-known language expert and professor of Arabic, Sylvestre de Sacy, they were intent on denigrating Maronite tenets. The Protestants were frustrated and disappointed with the local Christians who, not uncommonly, appeared to them as even more debased than Muslims.[23] Scholars felt the same way, too. Edward Robinson, founder of the field of biblical archaeology, discoverer of artifacts, and author of *Biblical Researches in Palestine* (1838), was repulsed by the Catholic and Orthodox "mummeries" that defile the Church of Holy Sepulcher. Local Christians were equally incensed by the Americans' arrogance. In 1823 the Maronite patriarch condemned the ingrate intruders as dangerous "Librati" or "Biblemen" who preached a "new blasphemy." The Catholics, meanwhile, demanded Ottoman protection against the Protestants' "false books" (*al-kutub al-batila*).[24] The Coptic patriarch told a missionary: "We had the Gospel before America was born."[25] Things would change for American missionaries in the future, particularly after they became an official "millet" within the Ottoman sphere in 1850, but they certainly were not embraced with open arms when they started out.

Although it would turn out to be a daunting and, in the end, impossible task to convert Muslims to Anglo-American Protestantism, or any Christian creed, for that matter, early accounts of Muslim conversion narratives fuelled hope throughout much of the nineteenth century and into the twentieth. *The Conversion of a Mahometan*, first published in the 1770s, went through seventeen editions, including one German translation in Pennsylvania. An essay about the secret conversion of one Muslim man (Abdallah), the betrayal by his friend Sabat to the Muslim authorities, who then tortured and executed Abdallah, the wandering of the guilt-ridden Sabat and his discovery of the New Testament in India, followed by his conversion and redemption was told by one Claudius Buchanan, a former chaplain in the British East India Company, in "The Star in the East" (1809). This story became a widespread sensation in the Anglo-American world, inspiring various theme-related works of art. One of the poems published during this time couldn't be more celebratory:

No more the Koran can its votaries warm,
No more Mahomet's paradise can charm;
When God who holds the destiny of man,
In his good time reveals his mighty plan.[26]

The story of As'ad Shidyaq, a Christian Maronite who was persecuted and imprisoned as a heretic because he converted to Protestantism, was used to inspire missionary work in the region. *The Life and Conversion of Mahomed Ali Bey*, first published in 1823, told the story of a Muslim convert disowned by his father, was later renamed Alexander Kazem Bey, and eventually taught Persian at St. Petersburg University. In his *The Setting of the Crescent and the Rising of the Cross* (1898), the influential Presbyterian missionary Henry Jessup recounted the story of Kamil Aierany—better known as Kamil Abdul Messiah after his conversion—who joined the missionary movement and died mysteriously in 1892. In the 1860s, quite a few Turkish converts ended up in jail, despite that nation's declared commitment to freedom of religion.[27]

Such success accounts were practically all the missionaries could claim in more than century of missionary activity, beginning with the pioneering mission of Pliny Fisk and Levi Parsons in 1819. Case after case of missionary enthusiasm ended up in disillusionment, as Muslims simply rejected the Protestant message. The great American writer, Herman Melville, had summarized the failure succinctly when he wrote in his *Journal of a Visit to Europe and the Levant* (1837) that American missionaries "might as well attempt to convert bricks into brick-cakes as the Orientals into Christians." "It is," he added, "against the will of God that the East should be Christianized."[28]

Shifting strategies, some believed that converting Eastern Christians, whose lax and corrupt ways gave a bad image of true Christianity, would be the best way to reach the target, but this strategy failed as well. This method was deemed unproductive by the Episcopal Horatio Southgate, in his treatise *Encouragement to Missionary Effort among Mohametans* (1836). Southgate, whose mission was independent from the American Board of Commission for Foreign Missions, or ABCFM, the missionary organization founded in 1810 to evangelize around the world, lamented the bad image the medieval crusades had left in the minds of Muslims. "The Church has sent against them . . . slaughtering armies . . . under the sacred banner of the Cross; but no messenger of love, bearing the glad tidings of peace and good-will." He ended up trying to find common ground between his tradition and that of the Eastern churches, thereby going against ABCFM's strategy.[29]

The lands of "Bible Christianity" (Syrian, Palestine, Lebanon, Turkey), occupied by Arab interlopers, were the primary target of ABCFM, but India, too, got its share of Anglo-American missionaries who paired Islam with Hinduism (a religion of idolatry) as twin evils. As denigrating views of locals kept pouring forth and evangelization struck a dead end, some, like Cyrus Hamlin, a longtime missionary in Turkey, concluded that only by laying the foundation of modern life could Christians eventually make progress. Others, like Henry Jessup, lamented the degraded status of Muslim women, a view taken up by Helen Barrett Montgomery in *Western Women in Eastern Lands* (1910).[30]

Anglo-American Protestant missionaries didn't give up, of course, and by 1906 organized a major conference in, of all places, Cairo, to be followed by others, including a major one in Edinburgh (1910) to launch a new global strategy of converting Muslims, one combining a social gospel (a secular *mission civilisatrice* based on introducing modernity to the Arab and Islamic worlds) with direct proselytization. This approach fit well with a number of prominent American missionaries and authors, chief among whom was Reformed Church evangelical and major author on Islam, Samuel Zwemer, "the most influential American Christian missionary to Muslims" in the first decades of the twentieth century, "if not ever," according to the Christian historian Thomas Kidd.[31] The dual mission of social uplift and conversion reflected his optimistic postmillennial disposition (Muslims convert before a millennium of peace is inaugurated to await the Messiah, not the more apocalyptic one of Christ's return, following a rapturous encounter in the sky with a group of elite believers, before a millennium of peace begins). Zwemer and his colleagues, like the Turkey-based James Barton, Foreign Secretary of the ABCFM and the India-based Presbyterian E. M. Wherry, all believed that Islam was their main rival for the souls of heathens around the world, that Islam was, basically, a failed religion, that the "Moslem peril" had to be defeated, and that, ultimately, in this cosmic battle for souls, "it is Islam or Christ!" Islam could certainly be defeated "with the Sword of the Spirit."

Some, like George Herrick, another missionary to Turkey, took a more conciliatory position toward Islam by rejecting the Christian crusading spirit in all its forms and finding possibilities of "a kind of universalist ecumenism," but this approach was too liberal even for Zwemer who seemed to believe that the last attempt to inject spirituality in Islam ended, strangely enough, with Mohammed al-Ghazali, the medieval Muslim scholar often blamed for stultifying independent thought in Islam by blacklisting philosophy. American missionaries were aggrieved by the Ottoman Sultan Abdul Hamid's massacre of the Christian Armenians between 1894 and 1896 and publicized the horrors back home, and though some were encouraged by the overthrow of the sultan by the "Young Turks" in 1908, the latter carried out the extermination in 1915. They organized relief operations worth millions of dollars in food and supplies, but they also were careful to separate Islam from the corrupt governments behind such massacres.[32]

In 1926 and 1927, R. C. Hutchinson, a philosophy professor in Iran writing in the pages of the *Atlantic Monthly*, regretted that Christians didn't show enough love to Muslims and said that Christian ministry doesn't have to depend on conversion to redeem Muslims. But in that age of rising Protestant fundamentalism, with its rejection of modernist tenets, such views had limited effect and faded rather quickly, giving way to the rise of conservative missions, more interested in the salvation of souls. Incidentally, Zwemer, then teaching at the Princeton Seminary and whose influence remained (and, apparently, has remained) immense, sided with the fundamentalist view because he came to realize that only thinking in "black and white" maintains orthodoxy.[33]

The euphoria over news of the seemingly mass conversion of Muslims in Indonesia in the mid-1960s was understandable given the failure and despair that had afflicted the American missionary movement in Muslim lands as a whole. J. N. D. Anderson, a former missionary in Egypt, admitted that Muslims were the "hardest nut we have to crack." Billy Graham called a major conference in 1974, held in Lausanne, Switzerland, in the spirit of the Cairo 1906 and Edinburgh 1910 conferences, to figure out, yet again, how to crack the Muslim nut. Other conferences followed, as missionaries tried to figure exactly how to approach the nagging question of Muslim conversion. Some recommended eschewing "cultural imperialism." An Argentine evangelist, Luis Bush, popularized a so-called "10/40 window," referring to the part of the globe, stretching from Africa to Japan, located between 10° and 40° latitude, and which is home to the largest concentration of Muslims in the world.[34]

When Muslim terrorists attacked the United States on September 11, 2001, President George W. Bush, even though he was a born-again Christian, did what all presidents do and maintained a strict separation between terrorists and Islam, the latter being, as he once said, a religion of peace. As we have seen before, the undiplomatic rhetoric was left to evangelists Pat Robertson, Franklin Graham, and Jerry Falwell, among many others. While the US Conference of Catholic Bishops counseled "deeper understanding and engage-ment with Islam," conservative Catholic Robert Spencer refused to mince his words and restated the old view that Islam itself is inher-ently violent. If Falwell had called Mohammed a terrorist (and later apologized), Jerry Vinces, former president of the Southern Baptist Convention, called the Prophet of Islam a "demon-possessed pedo-phile." Mohammed's marriage to Aisha, when she was six or nine, and regardless of whether the marriage was consummated at that age or not, was called by a California pastor "an act of pedophilia." Muslim converts to Protestantism wrote popular accounts unveiling the dark secrets of Islam, leading the brothers Ergun and Emir Caner to the position of dean in two different seminaries. The account of a former graduate of Al-Azhar University in Cairo, the foremost seat of Islamic learning in Sunni Islam, wrote under the pseudonym of Mark A. Gabriel. Because such Christians are inclined to see Islam as the source of violence and terrorism, one fringe Christian apolo-gist even recommend bombing all of Islam's holy sites, including the Ka'bah in Mecca and the Dome of the Rock in Jerusalem, as well as crackdown on immigrants, among other measures.

Islam was now interpreted as the Antichrist itself, a role it didn't have in earlier eschatological versions, although the Russians were the Muslims' allies in this apocalyptic scenario. Somehow, these Christians got wind of the role of the Mahdi in both Sunni and, especially, Shiite history, and that made the role fitting. One believer, Ralph Stice, even started a website titled "Mahdi Watch." This apocalyptic imaginary is quite complex, involving Russians, the attack of Gog and Magog as described in Ezekiel, and wars before the prophesied millennium dawns on our troubled world. (The Catholics, once the realm of evil and the Antichrist, have long since vanished from this Protestant script.) Such views found themselves into politics, with politicians like Oklahoma Senator James Inhofe urging support of Israel "because God said so," or because "this is God talking."[35] These statements and convictions, however, are not new; as Kidd reminds us, they are old themes updated to suit contemporary realities. Actually, the eschatological script seems to adapt to new political developments, and even seems to be dependent on them. Many Americans in our own day continue to read world events such as conflict, war, terrorism, and other atrocities as signs of an unfolding drama long foretold in the holy pages of the Bible.

Chapter 2

Holy Land for a Chosen People

From the very beginning, a significant number of American Protestants, like other members of the Western tradition, including, as we have seen, Columbus, acted as if the Holy Land, with its Holy Sepulcher, decreed by Emperor Constantine as the site of Jesus's crucifixion, was theirs by right. The only thing standing between them and that sacred place was Islam, or rather, the Ottoman Empire that ruled those lands until the early part of the twentieth century. The demise of the Ottomans was, therefore, anxiously anticipated because it was necessary for the fulfillment of the Protestant eschatological or millennialist vision. This vision, which has persisted to our own day, included the restoration of Jews to the land promised them in the Bible. God's promise to Abraham and the Hebrews was deemed by many prominent Protestant thinkers as final, absolute, and nonnegotiable.

Thus, at a very early stage in American history, we begin to see the contours of a polemic and a conflict that continue to affect American–Muslim relations today. Muslims the world over express sympathy for the Palestinians and wonder why the United States seems to be so unconditionally dedicated to the support of Israel. Explanations for this unfair state of affairs range from the power of the Israeli lobby in Washington to the failure of Arab or Muslim governments to separate themselves from the tutelage of the United States. Lobbies do have an impact, but there is obviously more to the story. The US support for Israel is simply part of a certain Anglo-American biblical worldview; it fits into a sequence of events that culminates with the sovereignty of Jews in the Holy Land, before they convert to Christianity and enter a new millennium of peace on Earth.

This Protestant script for Jews is a rather new development in Christian history. For early Roman Catholic Church fathers, Jews were heretics who had sinned and were, therefore, banished twice from the Promised Land. Their only salvation was through conversion, since the Rome-based Catholic Church, the New Israel, had become the site for God's promise. It was the Reformation—with its displacement of the Catholic Church and its emphasis on the Bible as the only way to connect with God's intent—that helped restore the Old Testament to Christian scripture. Despite Martin Luther's well-known anti-Semitic pronouncements that rival those of twentieth-century Nazi propagandists,[1] Luther's prejudices would be trumped by the text of the Bible, now reclaimed by Protestant believers from the hands of the Catholic Church.

The rediscovery of the Old Testament led to a revival in Hebrew and the Jewish wisdom found in Hebrew texts. And as Latin was being replaced by vernacular languages, Protestants, and, especially, Puritans, felt a deep kinship with the ancient Israelites, whose faith and ingenuity were seen as an inspiration to their own challenges. To be sure, Jews had long been yearning to regain their Promised Land, but when the Old Testament was incorporated into the Protestant outlook, identifying with the Holy Land and its ancient biblical stories became part of the Anglo Saxon theocratic mind. When looked at from the perspective of post-Reformation British and American histories, the creation of Israel and the ensuing struggles appear rather inevitable. In an ironic sort of way, the anti-Semite Luther launched a movement that culminated in the birth of Israel.

As early as 1649, two English Puritans residing in Amsterdam sent what is considered the first petition to the English government calling for human action to restore Jews to their Promised Land. They wanted England to "be the first and the readiest to transport Israel's sons and daughters on their ships to the land promised to their forefathers, Abraham, Isaac and Jacob for an everlasting inheritance."[2] Around the same time, Protestant Huguenots in France, Lutherans in Germany, and leaders in Denmark were making the same argument. In 1696, for instance, the Dane Holger Paulli called on the King of England, William III, to be "Cyrus the Great and the Almighty's instrument" in restoring Jews to their rightful land.[3] Paulli was referring to Cyrus the Great, the Persian emperor who restored Jews to their homeland in the sixth century B.C. and whose name has ever been evoked, as we shall see, in this context.

The English Puritan poet John Milton expressed the same sentiment in *Paradise Regained*. Many prominent European scientists and philosophers—such as Isaac Newton, Joseph Priestly, Jean-Jacques Rousseau, and Blaise Pascal—shared this view. Canonical English writers such as Lord Byron, Walter Scott, William Wordsworth, Robert Browning, and, especially, George Eliot, were all believers. They were convinced that the restoration of a Jewish state in Palestine would benefit the world. Political and military leaders made such beliefs easier to implement. In 1799, while on a military expedition in the Middle East, General Napoleon Bonaparte became the first statesman to propose a Jewish state in Palestine. From that time on, a regular stream of similar proposals were made across Europe and the United States. In 1840, Lord Palmerston, the British Foreign Secretary, asked Britain's ambassador in Constantinople to persuade the Ottoman authorities to help resettle Jews in Palestine and benefit from the Jews' industry, wealth, and loyalty:

> There exists at the present time among the Jews dispersed over Europe, a strong notion that the time is approaching when their nation is to return to Palestine. . . . It would be of manifest importance to the Sultan to encourage the Jews to return and to settle in Palestine because the wealth which they would bring with them would increase the resources of the Sultan's dominions; and the Jewish people, if returning under the sanction and protection and at the invitation of the Sultan, would be a check upon any future evil designs of Mehmet Ali [of Egypt] or his successor. . . I have to instruct Your Excellency strongly to recommend [to the Turkish Government] to hold out every just encouragement to the Jews to return to Palestine.[4]

Writing almost a century before the Balfour Declaration of 1917, Palmerston was expressing a widely held view of Jews as the most industrious and creative members of any society that hosts them. It was, in fact, partly for this reason that Jews would eventually embrace their own Zionism. They had come to realize that despite their contributions to their society, the ghosts of anti-Semitism couldn't be kept at bay, and that they could be the targets of hatred and oppression at any given time. Only a state of their own, where Jews would no longer be a vulnerable minority, could set them, and members of the Jewish Diaspora, free. Prominent Christians would not have disagreed. The influential Anglican minister William H. Hechter (1845–1931) wrote a treatise titled *The Restoration of the*

Jews to Palestine (1894) two years before Theodor Herzl published his *Der Judenstaat* (The Jewish State) in 1896. When Herzl opened his epoch-marking manifesto, he called for the *restoration*, not the creation, of a Jewish state.[5]

In 1853, when the future of the Ottoman Empire was in question during the Crimean War, the Seventh Earl of Shaftesbury—better known simply as Lord Shaftesbury—considered to be the greatest social reformer of the Victorian age, described Palestine as "a country without a nation" and Jews as a "nation without a country."[6] Variations of Shaftesbury's expression would be later repeated by the Anglo-Jewish writer Israel Zangwill, who popularized the notion of the United States as a "melting pot" and, of course, in the Balfour Declaration of 1917.

Such statements were not based on any empirical observation; they either meant something altogether different from what they have come to imply (there was, of course, no Palestinian nationality in that Ottoman province), or they were simply made in a vacuum. The land was certainly inhabited. Travelers to the Holy Land kept reporting that the place was heavily populated by Arabs who were attached to their native land. Ahad Ha'Am (born Asher Zvi Ginsberg), the leading spiritual Zionist of the late nineteenth century, visited Palestine and declared that Zionists must come to terms with the local Arab population. "We tend to believe abroad that Palestine is nowadays almost completely deserted," he wrote, "a non-cultivated wilderness, and anyone can come there and buy as much land as his heart desires. But in reality," Ha'Am added, "this is not the case. It is difficult to find anywhere in the country Arab land which lies fallow."[7] In 1898, after the first Zionist Congress was held, two Viennese rabbis reporting on Palestine said that the bride was indeed beautiful—the only problem, however, was that she was "married to another man."[8]

In the beginning, Lord Shaftesbury's views on Jews and Palestine were not taken too seriously; he was, for example, accused of madness by none other than the patron saint of nursing, Florence Nightingale—a healthy index of the influence of such religious movements at the time. Still, millennialist beliefs, whether in their postmillennial form (a new millennium of peace before the return of Christ) or the more strident premillennialist one (Christ in person returns to Earth to usher in a new millennium of peace and harmony) and restorationist ideas gained more respectability in the course of the nineteenth century, including in the United States, where such religious disposition blended seamlessly with the nation's secular ethos.[9]

This is not to say that Christian Zionists were driven by the noblest of sentiments toward Jews. There was, in fact, a very fine line between restorationism and classical anti-Semitism, particularly in the later Victorian and Edwardian periods, because by insisting on conversion, Christian Zionists affirmed the different nature of the Jewish people. This is why many Jews opposed Christian Zionism. By elevating Jews, Christian Restorationists were also consigning them to their natural homeland in Palestine. The historian Goldwin Smith saw restoration as a solution to Europe since the Jews were alien to European civilization. In James Blyth's novels, *The Tyranny* (1907) and *Ichabod* (1910), the Jews are deported out of Britain to Mexico and Latin America, although one of the heroes suggests boating them out "in a jiffy" and sending them "home to Jericho."[10] Even when Arthur Balfour, who, like six of the nine members of the British War Cabinet, was from an evangelical religious background, issued his sixty-seven-word Declaration on November 2, 1917, he was opposed by the only Jewish member of that Cabinet, Edwin Samuel Montagu. In a separate memorandum, Montagu considered the document anti-Semitic for singling Jews out as a separate "nation" or "people" whose natural homeland was in Palestine.[11] As a member of a generations-old English family, Montagu rejected the notion that a "Jewish Englishman and a Jewish Moor" were somehow members of one nation, while a "Christian Englishman and a Christian Frenchman" were not. This was all the more troubling for Montagu because, historically, Christianity has claimed as much a right to the Holy Land as any other religion does, including Judaism and Islam. Montagu was not the only Jew to see through the anti-Semitism in Balfour's Declaration. Jewish Zionists also accused the author of the Declaration of anti-Semitism when he opposed Jewish immigration into Britain.[12]

In the United States, one might say that the restorationist impulse, which almost always implies the defeat of Islam, has never faded entirely and, as in England, was galvanized by the decline of the Ottoman Empire. As the historian James Field reported, the American publication *Nile's Register* noted in 1816 that if Jews were to "unite their efforts, they might well overcome the weak and imbecile Ottoman Empire, the degraded East might again become the seat of commerce and the arts, and the desert bloom like the rose."[13] On October 31, 1819, the twenty-five-year-old Protestant missionaries, Levi Parsons and Pliny Fisk, announced in Boston's Old South Church that the time had come to restore Jews to their homeland in Palestine in anticipation of the Second Coming. When Levi Parsons died less than five years later, a requiem celebrated him with such lines: "Thy spirit, Parsons, lur'd by seraph's song/ . . . who like him [shall] destroy Mohammed's sway?"[14] The same year Parsons and Fisk left for the Middle East (1819), ex-president John Adams received a copy of the book, *Travels in England, France, Spain and the Barbary States*, written by the Jewish writer, politician, and diplomat, Mordecai Noah. The eighty-four-year-old Adams wished that Noah "had been at the head of a hundred thousand Israelites . . . marching with them into Judea & making a conquest of that country & restoring your nation to the dominion of it. For I really wish the Jews again in Judea an independent nation." Adams' statement, according to the American Jewish Historical Society, was "the first pro-Zionist declaration by an American head of state, active or retired."[15]

By the middle of the nineteenth century, naval officers like William Francis Lynch, who sailed down the Jordan River with metallic boats all the way to the Sea of Galilee, thought that resettling Jews in Palestine would be good for the region and the world. American Methodists, Congregationalists, and Presbyterians, as well as prominent Americans like the historian George Bush (ancestor to President George W. Bush) and Joseph Smith, founder of Mormonism, would have agreed with Lord Shaftesbury's slogan that Palestine was "a land without a people for a people without land."[16]

The Philadelphian Millerite Clorinda Minor, editor of *Advent Messenger of the Daughters of Zion* and author of *Meshullam! Or, Tidings from Jerusalem* (1851), wanted to restore Palestine to its biblical status, which meant converting Jews as a prerequisite condition for the Apocalypse. The Mormon elder Orson Hyde, author of *A Voice From Jerusalem* (1842) believed that America is connected to ancient Israelites prayed for a leader to help the Jews reclaim their lost land:

> Thou, O Lord, did once move upon the heart of Cyrus to shew favor unto Jerusalem and her children. Do thou now also be pleased to inspire the hearts of kings and the powers of the earth to look with a friendly eye toward this place and with a desire to see their righteous purposes executed in relation thereto. Let them know that it is thy good pleasure to restore the kingdom unto Israel—raise up Jerusalem as its capital, and constitute her people as a distinct nation and government.[17]

Another Philadelphian, Warder Cresson, abandoned a comfortable farm life, including a wife and eight children, sailed for Palestine with a dove, converted to Judaism, renamed himself Michael C. Boaz Israel and got circumcised for the occasion, published a book (*The Key of David*), married a Jewess, and fathered two more children before he died in 1860. In the process, he dismissed the whole of Christianity (not just Roman Catholicism and the Greek Orthodox church) as "the whore of Babylon."[18]

When Americans visited the Holy Land they often did with strong preconceptions about the place and its history. Many experienced the journey as a pilgrimage, some even retracing the route of Israelites across the Sinai desert. One American woman from Baltimore, Maryland, Annie DeWitt Shaw, wrote a letter in the summer of 1859 expressing the commonly held view that the Jews' restoration to the Holy Land is indispensable for the fulfillment of prophecy:

> The Jews' wailing place was to me the most interesting place in Jerusalem. My dragoman, an East Indian Jew, of Moorish skin, who, by the way, is an English subject, and speaks English well, conducted me thither. We threaded our way through the usual narrow and dirty lanes, misnamed streets, of Eastern cities, and came to an area in the form of a quadrangle, near the bridge where the dwellers in Zion were once wont to pas over, to worship God in the Temple on His holy mount, Moriah. In the ancient foundation wall of the Temple are several courses of large, leveled stones, upon which the Jews lavish their kisses and embraces and through the crevices of which they pour up their prayers to God for the restoration of His Temple, and their early coming triumph in Jerusalem.[19]

In 1858, American doctor and missionary J. T. Barclay published a book titled *The City of the Great King: Jerusalem As It Was, As It Is, and As It Is To Be*. Declaring that the "days of Islamism are numbered," as foreign consuls were granted more powers to govern local Christians, he was confident that Jews were headed toward a more promising future. "A better day has already dawned upon Zion," he wrote.[20] J. V. C. Smith, author of *A Pilgrimage to Palestine*, echoed the same sentiments:

> As frequently expressed in the course of preceding observations on the future destiny of the Land of Promise, I fully believe in the final restoration of the Jews, and the re-establishment of the nation. That

greatest of all events to the reflecting Christian, who sees the hand of God in the eventful history of the descendants of Abraham, must be brought about by the concurrence and guarantee of all the Christian powers of the earth, who will thus be instrumentalities in fulfilling the intentions of Divine Providence.[21]

The Holy Land was, in a way, the common property of all Christians and Bible readers. What the biblical archeologist Edward Robinson wrote could have been said by thousands, if not millions, of his fellow citizens:

As in the case of most of my countrymen, especially in New England, the scenes of the Bible had made a deep impression upon my mind from the earliest childhood. . . . Indeed in no country in the world, perhaps, is such a feeling more widely diffused than in New England; in no country are the Scriptures better known, or more highly prized. From his earliest years the child is there accustomed not only to read the Bible for himself, but he reads or listens to it in the morning and evening devotions of the family, in the daily village school, in the Sunday school and Bible class, and in the weekly ministrations of the sanctuary.[22]

Such sense of ownership only added to the sense of insult and injury, when such pilgrim travelers encountered the barbaric Muslim landlords. One Josiah Brewer predicted that

a holier cross than that borne by the crusaders, shall take the place of the crescent which we now see around us, on the top of the minarets; and instead of the blood-red flag, with its drawn sword in the midst, there shall float on these walls, the white banner and branch of peace.[23]

In 1863, President Abraham Lincoln agreed with a Canadian clergyman who told him that there would be no peace in the world until the long-persecuted Jews were restored to their homeland in Palestine. Lincoln thought that would be "a noble dream and one shared by many Americans."[24]

Not long after the Civil War, veterans were leading Arabs against Ottomans and pressing Arab rulers to respect their rights of their Jewish subjects. There was growing consensus to bring spiritual and secular light to Middle East, a prospect that fired the hopes of American Jews. Shocked by Russia's pogroms of 1881, Emma

Lazarus, the poet of Sephardic ancestry, praised by Ralph Waldo Emerson, Henry James, and Walt Whitman, was awakened to the "Jewish problem" and wanted Palestine to be "a home for the homeless, a goal for the wanderer, an asylum for the persecuted, a nation for the denationalized." Palestine, to Lazarus, was the solution to oppressed Jews, not American ones, for the latter were blessed to live in a free country. Israel would be a blessing to Jews and the world, she believed.

Lazarus's was a lonely voice, however. Most Americans did not subscribe to Lazarus's Zionist philosophy, mostly because it was tricky to do so in a world where anti-Semitism was very much alive and where Jews, as the conservative scholar Abram S. Isaacs told the poet, were still seen as "only Palestinians, Semites, [and] Orientals." Though not ardent Zionists, American Jews, however, gave generously to the cause. The benevolence of Nathan Straus, Macy's cofounder, is now honored in the name of the city of Netanya in Israel.[25]

In 1891, the wealthy Chicago evangelical William Blackstone had 413 prominent Americans, including J. P. Morgan, John D. Rockefeller, and Charles Scribner, as well as the editors of the *Chicago Tribune* and the *New York Times*, sign a petition (known as the Blackstone Memorial) calling on President Benjamin Harrison to be "a modern Cyrus to help restore the Jews to Zion," but such calls remained unheeded, partly because restorationism had mellowed (although it was still widespread) and the Ottomans were opposed. Blackstone reissued the call in 1916 with the support of Jewish Zionists, and sent it to President Wilson. It was, therefore, not without reason that Nathan Straus told Blackstone that Supreme Court Justice Louis Dembitz Brandeis, the son of Bohemian Jews who rose to become one of the most distinguished progressive lawyers of his time and the first Jew to be appointed to the US Supreme Court, believed that he was the Father of Zionism since Blackstone's work "antedates Herzl."[26]

Zionism was not nearly as popular in the United States as it was in Europe, partly because American Jews feared an outburst of anti-Semitism and Orthodox Jews were against the secular tenets of Zionism, but the zeal of American Jews like Kiev-born and Milwaukee resident Golda Mabovitz (later Meyerson, and then Meir) and the general Jewish support of resettling East European Jews in Palestine kept the momentum going. The support of Louis Brandeis also gave

the Zionist cause more visibility. In this way, the American Zion
came to the rescue of the biblical one.

Prominent Americans were drafted in the cause. "It seems to me
entirely proper to start a Zionist State around Jerusalem," declared
Theodore Roosevelt, for peace would only happen if Jews were
given Palestine and both Jews and Arabs were granted independence.[27] When Balfour, the British Foreign Secretary, came to the
United States in April 1917 seeking the commitment of Woodrow
Wilson and his administration, the American president rejected Balfour's proposal for an Anglo-American administration of the Holy
Land because Wilson was, in principle, against imperialism. His
foreign policy adviser Colonel Edward Mandell House even stated
that such a scheme would make the Middle East "a breeding place
for future war." But Balfour, undeterred and convinced by Brandeis
that Wilson was actually sympathetic to the Zionist cause, made his
declaration on November 2, 1917. Wilson may have been opposed
to imperialism, but his sympathy for the restoration of Jews to Palestine was, like many of his Anglo-Americans, part of his religious
upbringing.[28] Wilson explained his support for the Balfour Declaration by exclaiming: "To think that I, the son of the manse, should
be able to help restore the Holy Land to its people."[29] Michael Oren
describes the aftermath of the Declaration:

> Jews throughout the world believed that it could not have been formu-
> lated without Wilson's consent. A crowd of 100,000 Jews reportedly
> danced in gratitude outside the U.S. consulate in Odessa, with smaller
> demonstrations occurring in front of legations in Greece, China, and
> Australia. Telegrams of thanks billowed into the White House.[30]

The Jewish Legion, founded by Vladimir Jabotinsky, was allowed
to recruit in the United States, which was how Nehemia Rabin, father
to Yitzhak, joined. For the first time in two thousand years, the Jews
had a military force and a flag. Although Zionists like Brandeis didn't
think the Arabs were a serious obstacle to a Jewish state in Palestine,
many prominent Jews, including Henry Morgenthau, the prominent
Wilson supporter, were opposed to US involvement. Some foresaw
trouble and strife. William Yale, the State Department's special agent
in the Middle East, knew that "if a Jewish State is to be created in Palestine it will have to be done by force of arms and maintained by force
of arms amid an overwhelmingly hostile population."[31]

Despite such warnings and admonitions, Wilson publicly announced his support for the Zionist project in 1918. Following the Paris Peace Conference of 1919, Yale, member of a fact-finding team, now thought that a Jewish state represented "American ideals and American civilization" and would benefit the whole region. It was, as Oren puts it, "an astonishing volte-face of views,"[32] one that did not change the truth of his earlier prediction. More realistic and perhaps emblematic of the general American sentiment regarding Jews was John F. Kennedy. When the future president was a senior at Harvard, he proposed a solution that turned out to be rather insightful: "It seems to me," he wrote, "that the only thing to do will be to break the country [Palestine] into two autonomous districts."[33]

The Nazi regime in Germany increased the momentum for a decision. Franklin D. Roosevelt (FDR) favored a Jewish state, but he was also fearful of what he called "a Holy Gehad." The American Golda Meyerson moved to Palestine and eventually became prime minister (1969–1974). Baltimore-born Henrietta Szold, founder of the Hadassah, believed that "Arab-Jewish relationships should have been the central point of our Zionist thinking."[34] She introduced Arabic in Jewish school curricula and held on to the vision of a binational state. So did Oakland-born Judah Leib Magnes, later to become chancellor and president of Hebrew University. Against Arab and Jewish obduracy, the pacifist believed that "there is a better chance of averting . . . bloodshed if we make every possible effort . . . to work hand in hand—as teachers, helpers, friends—with this awakening Arab world."[35]

Undeterred by US wavering and neutrality, Zionists brought in the hydrologist Elwood Mead and soil specialist Dr. Walter Clay Lowdermilk to help revive the long-degraded land of Palestine. In 1940, Hillel Kook (known as Peter Bergson) arrived in the United States and placed hundreds of ads in major newspapers like the *New York Times*, lobbied for bipartisan support in Congress, and drafted Hollywood celebrities like Frank Sinatra, Jerry Lewis, and Marlon Brando into the Zionist cause. Two years later, in 1942, at New York City's Biltmore Hotel, Zionists agreed on creating a Jewish state in Palestine and that the United States, not the United Kingdom, would henceforth constitute the "battleground" over which the battle would be fought.[36]

Meanwhile, the Palestine conundrum remained unresolved. When FDR chose his own man, the general, attorney, and diplomat Patrick J. Hurley, to survey nationalist movements in the North Africa and the Middle East, Hurley told David Ben-Gurion that America was not bound by "Jewish interpretations of Old Testament verses,"[37] and when FDR met with Ibn Saud aboard the Quincy on Valentine Day, 1945, the Arab king warned the American president about the consequences of supporting Zionism in Palestine and recommended that the Germans pay for the horrors inflicted on Jews. "Amends should be made by the criminal, not the innocent bystander," the King emphasized. FDR changed his mind, claiming that the American people had been "misinformed" about the situation, which only disappointed the Zionists.[38]

Although many missionaries read the rise of Israel through traditional eschatological lenses, those working in the Middle East realized early on that the establishment of Israel and the displacement of Arabs had hardened feelings against Christians and the West. The Anglican bishop in Cairo and Jerusalem Kenneth Cragg, whose book, *The Call of the Minaret* (1956), is still in print, blamed Zionism for the treatment of Arab Muslims in Palestine.[39]

A few theologically liberal Christians, such as the former president of Union Theological Seminary, Henry Sloan Coffin, Sr., warned in 1947 that American support for Israel was fueling a "violent anti-American feeling" because Americans were seen as "aggressive meddlers" and "hypocrites." But the belief that Israel is bound to return to the biblical land of Canaan, which stretched beyond Israel's 1948 boundaries, continued to enjoy solid support. In 1958, the liberal theologian Reinhold Neibuhr described the new state of Israel as a "glorious moral and political achievement." When it became clear that international political community would not give Israel a free expansionist hand in the region following the 1956–1957 war, William Hull, the Canadian Pentecostal missionary and author of *Israel: Key to Prophecy* (1957), introduced the element of rapture and reintroduced the Muslim Roman Catholic unholy alliance of the long-gone historicist eschatology teaming up against the Jews.[40]

It would be the fate of Baptist-raised Harry S. Truman, a restorationist who was moved by Jewish suffering to be faced with making the decision. By 1947, he had already contained Soviet designs on North Africa and the Middle East and dispatched the Naval Forces Mediterranean (renamed later the Sixth Fleet) to the Eastern Mediterranean, but nothing wore him down more than the Palestine issue. He would complain repeatedly about the Zionist pressure on him at home, explain that he didn't have "hundreds of thousands of Arabs in my constituents,"[41] but he also pressured Great Britain into loosening its immigration and land-purchase restrictions.

Several commissions recommended trusteeship and partition, with Jerusalem under some international mandate. Each recommendation, however, ignited a storm, often uniting Zionists and Arabs in the Middle East in protests against the US government. Truman was worried that support for a Jewish state might drive Arabs into Soviet arms, but when the Soviet Union, more interested in dislodging Great Britain from the Middle East, announced its support for partition, the Zionists put more pressure on Truman. And when Truman embargoed all arms sales to the Middle East, the Zionists managed to raise funds from Hollywood celebrities like Frank Sinatra and underworld figures like Bugsy Siegel. The Haganah, armed with new Czech weapons, attacked Arabs and massacred civilians, leading to the flight of terrorized Palestinians. On May 14, 1947, David Ben-Gurion, Golda Meir and others, assembled in the Tel Aviv Museum, announced independence. (The British had announced their plan to withdraw.) That same evening, Truman, with practically no options left, extended US recognition to "the provisional government as the de facto authority of the State of Israel." Despite his doubts and fears, Truman was credited by American Jews as the president who helped create Israel, although Truman saw himself more as a latter-day Cyrus the Great.[42]

The victory of Israel over its Arab neighbors in the Six-Day War of 1967 and its capture of the Golan Heights, West Bank, Gaza Strip, the Sinai Peninsula and, most importantly, Jerusalem, was nothing less than a miracle and "the fulfillment of Jesus's prophecy in Luke 21–24 about Jerusalem being trod down until the 'times of the Gentiles' had expired."[43] The Jews hadn't controlled the Holy City since 597 B.C., Wilbur Smith reminded readers of his *Israel/Arab Conflict* (1967). As had been done many times before, the drama was, in some instances, read through the prism of the Isaac/Ishmael rivalry, with the latter's resentment driving Arab and Muslim anti-Semitism. A voice here and there cautioned against the impact of Israel's behavior on Muslim–American relations, but the apocalyptic view was getting even more popular. With the writings of Hal Lindsay, an evangelist with Campus Crusade for Christ and, in the 1990s, Tim LaHaye's *Left Behind* series, the image of Muslims as an obstacle to prophecy intensified. The Dome of the Rock was now seen standing in the way of rebuilding the temple and an earthquake was anticipated to topple it. Another scenario had Arab Muslims allying with the Soviets before both are destroyed.

The brief spotlight on the conflicted relationship between Americans and Muslims—or, if one prefers, the United States and the Middle East—outlined in the previous pages shows that there is obviously a long and deeply rooted history, albeit not a mainstream one, of American enthusiasm for the Holy Land and support for the restoration of Jews in it. Many Muslims and Arabs do read the American and West's sense of entitlement to their native land as a new crusade couched in the language of biblical prophecy. This perception doesn't help Americans and Muslims reach out to each other, nor does it help Israelis and Palestinians forge a durable peace. Still, it might be useful to distinguish the motives of American Protestants from those of medieval Catholic crusaders. American Protestants despised Roman Catholicism for the longest time, as that faith was considered to be the realm of the Antichrist that had to be vanquished before the new millennium. The early Protestant missionaries to the Middle East expressed horror at the medieval Crusades that, incidentally, targeted Muslims and Jews indiscriminately, and many considered the Catholics to have done irreparable damage for their later evangelical mission among Muslims. The Protestants were engaged in a spiritual conquest, one of souls, not bodies. They were the "artillery of heaven," not the armies of the pope, if you will. If there was any violence in their enterprise, it was strictly spiritual. "The instinct of the Crusaders was right, although their method was wrong," is how the influential Samuel Zwemer put it more than century later.[44] This still doesn't change the Muslim suspicion of Christian hostility, whether Catholic or Protestant, to their religion; but, at least, this is what American Protestants believed.

As uncomfortable as they may make us, the vitriolic comments that were made about Islam in the aftermath of 9/11, or the ones yet to come from evangelicals and other Christian fundamentalists, are part of America's intellectual tradition. The longing for the Holy Land as a place of freedom and redemption, whether it implies the defeat and conversion of local Muslims and Christians and the restoration of Jews or not, is a staple of the American spiritual imagination. America's unshakeable support for Israel is not merely the expression of a cynical policy dictated by lobbies and strategic interests, unless one defines interests as cultural affinities. Leading theologians like Reinhold Neibuhr and Paul Tillich, trade unions such as the American Federation of Labor (AFL), the US Congress, and every US president since Woodrow Wilson supported the creation of a Jewish state in Palestine.[45] Lyndon Johnson could have spoken for all Americans when he told the Jewish organization B'nai B'rith: "The Bible stories are woven into my childhood memories as the gallant struggle of modern Jews to be free of persecution is woven into our souls."[46] To be sure, many prominent early twentieth-century American Jews, such Bernard M. Baruch, remained suspicious, if not hostile, to Zionism,[47] but they had little effect on the course of history.

It is, therefore, perfectly understandable for Jerry Falwell to claim that his Old Testament made him a reliable Zionist.[48] "The destiny of the State of Israel," Falwell said in a 1984 interview, "is without question the most crucial international matter facing the world today. I believe that the people of Israel have not only a theological but also a historical and legal right to the land. I am personally a Zionist, having gained that perspective from my belief in Old Testament scriptures."[49] Falwell's influence among American Christians was so highly appreciated by Israeli leaders that when Israel bombed an Iraqi nuclear plant in 1981, Prime Minister Menachem Begin informed him before he did President Reagan.[50] For Falwell, and millions of Protestants like him, support for Israel is part of the faith. Less than two years after 9/11, General William Boykin, Deputy Under-Secretary of Intelligence, addressing a church congregation, said:

> And we ask ourselves this question, "Why do they hate us? Why do they hate us so much?" Ladies and gentlemen, the answer to that is because we're a Christian nation, because our foundation and our roots are Judeo-Christian. Did I say Judeo-Christian? Yes. Judeo-Christian. That means we've got a commitment to Israel. That means it's a commitment we're never going to abandon. We, in the army of God, in the house of God, in the kingdom of God, have been raised for such a time as this.[51]

During a three-day visit in 2009 to support a settler movement in Israel, Rabbi Eliezer Melamed, upon hearing about Mike Huckabee's views on Israel, said, "We hope that under Mike Huckabee's presidency, he will be like Cyrus and push us to rebuild the Temple and bring the final redemption."[52] We don't have to agree with such religious beliefs, but neither can we ignore their resonance in the

American cultural and political mind. The restoration of Jews to
the land God promised them in the Bible is a deeply ingrained part
of American culture and explains much of the US government's
position on the Israeli–Palestinian conflict that has consumed Jews,
Arabs, Muslims, and, indeed, the whole world for close to a century now. Therefore, if we are serious about seeking peace in the
Middle East, we can't afford not to address this aspect of Protestant
theology. Fervor for the apocalypse is not the surest way to foster
goodwill among Americans and Muslims. Just as Muslims will have
to take a hard look at their traditions and beliefs, so must those evangelical Christians who are committed to Biblical literalism. I will say
more about this later in the book.

Chapter 3

How Islam Shaped America

Saving souls and restoring Jews to their long-promised land were not the only ways to approach Arabs and Muslims. Many other Americans, including missionaries and travelers to the Holy Land, as well as politicians and writers, were able to maintain a more complex view of Islam and its lands. President Obama's conciliatory approach to the United States' conflict with Muslim-majority nations also has echoes in American history. American prejudices about Islam were sometimes tempered by the realization that Arabs and Muslims had given much to the West and that Muslim practices were, in some cases, like in the treatment of slaves, even superior.

I mentioned before that captivity narratives in the seventeenth, eighteenth, and nineteenth centuries were used as literary devices to promote the supremacy of the Protestant faith and American patriotism, but some Americans used this early encounter with—and knowledge of—Muslims not to condemn Islam but to chastise America itself. While the country was outraged that a few Muslim rogue states along the Mediterranean had captured their fellow (mostly white) countrymen and were keeping them in slave-like conditions, these Americans wondered why their nation, which enslaved far more blacks, didn't seem to be troubled by that fact.

When, in 1700, the Massachusetts Puritan judge Samuel Sewall printed the first antislavery tract in New England, he pointed out to the hypocrisy of his nation: "Methinks, when we are bemoaning the barbarous Usage of our Friends and Kinsfolk in Africa: it might not be unseasonable to enquire whether we are not culpable in forcing the Africans to become Slaves amongst our selves."[1] In 1776, when few Americans were held captive in Barbary, the Congregational minister Samuel Hopkins used the pulpit of his church, in Newport, Rhode Island, to argue that if Americans didn't condemn slavery at home, then the "Africans have a good right to make slaves of us and our children. . . . And the Turks have a good right to all the Christian slaves they have among them; and to make as many more slaves of us and our children, as shall be in their power. . . . According to this, every man has a warrant to make a bond slave of his neighbor, whenever it lies in his power." And in 1786, John Jay, foreign-affairs secretary of the nascent nation, asked whether the difference between American slaves at home and those abroad was due to the fact "that the American slaves at Algiers were WHITE people, whereas the African slaves at New York were BLACK people." At the Philadelphia Convention of 1787, the Abolition Society of Pennsylvania stated: "Providence seems to have ordained the sufferings of our American brethren, groaning in captivity in Algiers, to awaken to a sentiment of the injustice and cruelty of which we are guilty towards the wretched Africans."[2]

The influence of Islam on the issue of freedom and religion in the United States continued into the nineteenth century. At the age of twelve, a black slave in Baltimore by the name of Frederick Bailey (considered to be a corruption of the Islamic name Bilal), read a two-act play titled *Slaves in Barbary* and was impressed by the character of an enlightened Muslim ruler who condemns the evils of slavery. Frederick later escaped, changed his last name to Douglass, and wrote his own slave narrative, *The Life and Times of Frederick Douglass*.[3] This book is now a classic of American as well as abolitionist literature, and is taught all over the world.

The narrative of James Riley, a white American sailor, also showcased the more humane aspects of Islamic culture to Americans. In 1815, James Riley and members of his crew were shipwrecked on the coast of Africa and taken prisoner by a band of Bedouins. Sidi Hamet (Ahmed), a Moroccan trader, ransomed Riley and a few of his companions from impending death. The benevolence of this Muslim man so moved the American readers of Riley's bestselling story that in 1822, Elijah Brown, a prominent South Carolinian, wrote to Riley informing him that he had named his youngest son Sidi Hamet in honor of the Moroccan trader.[4] Riley himself, commenting on the philosophy of another humanitarian Moroccan, Rais bel Cossim, wrote: "To hear such sentiments from the mouth of a Moor, whose nation I had been taught to consider the worst of barbarians, I confess, filled my mind with awe and reverence, and I looked up to him as a kind of superior being, when he added, 'We are all children of the same heavenly Father, who watches over all our actions, whether we be Moor, or Christian, or Pagan, or any other religion; we must perform his will.'"[5] When Abraham Lincoln was running for president in 1860, he was asked about the books that had influenced him most. He named six, one of which was James Riley's personal story of captivity.[6]

Muslim Morocco also played an official role in US history. As President Obama noted in his famous Cairo speech on June 4, 2009, Morocco was the first country to recognize the independence of the United States, explicitly extending to it the same maritime and commercial privileges given other friendly nations. In 1780, Congress wrote the Moroccan sultan expressing its gratitude and assuring him of "every protection and assistance to your subjects from the people of these states whenever and wherever they may have it in their power." Soon after being elected president in 1789, George Washington sent a letter to Mohammed Ben Abdellah, the "Emperor of Morocco," his "Great and magnanimous Friend," thanking him for Morocco's friendship and promising the monarch that someday the United States would be helpful to its friends. Washington said that "while I remain at the head of this nation, I shall not cease to promote every measure that may conduce to the Friendship and Harmony" between Morocco and the United States "and shall esteem myself happy in every occasion of convincing your Majesty of the high sense (which in common with the whole nation) I entertain of the Magnanimity, Wisdom, and Benevolence of your Majesty."[7]

American literature of the period touched on Islam as well. In 1797, Royall Tyler published *The Algerine Captive*, one of the first American novels to consciously part ways with British sensibilities and affirm the new nation's revolutionary values. When Tyler's Yankee protagonist, Doctor Underhill, is held captive in Algiers, his faith is challenged by a smart "mollah," but he never gives in and turns renegade. Instead, the doctor sets out to understand Muslims. After noting that Islam has nothing to do with the cruel behavior of his captors, he says,

> I cannot help noticing it as extraordinary, that the Mahometan should abominate the christian on account of his faith, and the christian detest

the Mussulman for his creed; when the koran of the former acknowl-
edges the divinity of the christian Messias, and the bible of the latter
commands us to love our enemies. If each would follow the obvious
dictates of his own scripture, he would cease to hate, abominate, and
destroy the other.[8]

Tyler concludes his remarkable novel by warning the US government not to let "foreign emissaries inflame us against one nation, by
raking up the ashes of long extinguished enmity."[9]

As scholars Timothy Marr and Brian Yothers have shown, inherited views of Islam were soon tempered by travel accounts and
missionary reports from Arab and Muslim lands. On the issues of
slavery and temperance, despotic Muslims were seen the moral supe-
riors, showing more humanity and commonsense than the Enlightened Christians of America. As national confidence rose, curiosity
replaced fear. Oriental fashions were adopted and travelers sent less
biased (although not necessarily flattering) messages about the Holy
Land and the Middle East as a whole.

Herman Melville's eighteen-thousand-line poem *Clarel, A Poem
and Pilgrimage in the Holy Land*, published in 1876 after two
decades of continuous and assiduous work, capped decades of thinking about religion, the Holy Land, and American culture. No place
was more likely to disappoint than Palestine, particularly Jerusalem,
Melville had written in 1856. By the time he visited the Holy Land
in 1857, pilgrimage had become a mere form of religious tourism,
with sacred places competing for attention with other more prosaic
buildings. He ridiculed the mania for restorationism and the religious
obsessions of the American pilgrims and visitors.[10] Echoing the language of tour guides in Jerusalem, Melville summed up the feeling
in two sentences: "Here is the stone Christ leaned against, and here
is the English hotel. Yonder is the arch where Christ was shown to
the people, and just by that open window is sold the best coffee in
Jerusalem." The Church of the Holy Sepulcher was nothing more
than "sickening cheat."[11] Melville's verdict grew worse. He thought
that his fellow Anglo-Saxons are no more entitled to sacredness
than are the inhabitants of the Holy Land, including the oft-cursed
Muslims.[12]

Another quintessential American writer, Ralph Waldo Emerson,
read broadly across Muslim history and culture and, although shaped
by America's long antagonism toward Islam, tried to transcend

cultural prejudices and narrow beliefs by reaching out for common ground and understanding. He was inspired by Persian poetry and Arab wisdom, read the Qu'ran, and quoted the Prophet as an advocate of good learning on more than one occasion. In his 1850 essay "Representative Men," Emerson wrote:

> The Koran makes a distinct class of those who are by nature good, and whose goodness has an influence on others, and pronounces this class to be the aim of creation: the other classes are admitted to the feast of being, only as following in the train of this. And the Persian poet exclaims to a soul of this kind, "Go boldly forth, and feast on being's banquet; Thou are the called, the rest admitted with thee.[13]

The great American Transcendentalist may, in fact, have been influenced by the Persian Islamic philosophy he read in *Akhlak-i-Jalaly,* a medieval text translated by W. F. Thompson in 1839 as *The Practical Philosophy of the Muhammadan People,* a book that did much to dispel negative stereotypes of Islam and Muslims.[14] The influence of Islam on Emerson, as shown in his 1860 collection of essays, *The Conduct of Life,* considered to be his best work, is unmistakable:

> The religion which is to guide and fulfill the present and coming ages, whatever else it be, must be intellectual. The scientific mind must have a faith which is science. "There are two things," said Mahomet, "which I abhor, the learned in his infidelities, and the fool in his devotions." Our times are impatient of both, and specially of the last. Let us have nothing now which is not its own evidence.[15]

Toward the end of his life, Emerson echoed Rais bel Cossim, the Moroccan man in James Riley's captivity account: "In matters of religion," Emerson wrote, "men eagerly fasten their eyes on the differences between their creed and yours, whilst the charm of the study is in finding the agreements and identities in all the religions of men."[16] Thoreau was similarly impressed. Reflecting on the great Persian poet Saadi in his journal, he wrote: "I can find no essential difference between Saadi and myself. He is not Persian—he is not ancient—he is not strange to me."[17]

James Riley's narrative, Royall Tyler's novel, Emerson's philosophy, and Melville's wisdom show that contact with different people and knowledge of their traditions help dispel prejudices and create openings for dialogue and friendship. James Riley came out of his ordeal with a stronger appreciation for the great principles of the American Revolution, but he also learned that both Muslims and Americans are part of a common humanity, as he discovered that each culture had a lot to teach the other. Such Americans knew how to combine their sense of uniqueness and privilege without playing down the value of other traditions.

If the United States, through its missionaries and even through its business-minded entrepreneurs, did much to enrich Middle Eastern lands in the last two centuries, Muslims and Arabs have also made significant contributions to American culture and civilization. The religion of Islam may have repelled Christians and secular freedom lovers, but its culture also intrigued and fascinated them. One can understand Americans giving biblical names to their children, towns, and cities, but why would Elijah Boardman, a Revolutionary War hero and US senator, name a town Medina, in Ohio? In 1848, Phineas Taylor Barnum, one of America's first millionaires, finished building Iranistan, a dreamlike personal house in Bridgeport, Connecticut, inspired by Islamic or Moorish architecture. It lasted long enough for him to entertain the greatest writers of the time and attract the world-famous Swedish singer and soprano, Jenny Lind, to come perform in the United States. (Lind was heard by a visiting Turkish dignitary during a rare visit in 1850.[18]) By the time the mansion burned to the ground in 1857, the booking of the Swedish star had made up for the cost of construction.

Soon, the Moorish Revival style swept across America. I remember being stunned at the almost surreal sight of the Fox Theater in Atlanta, Georgia, when I visited that city for the first time in 2006. At the height of America's war on Islamic terrorism and the war in Iraq, there stood a huge structure that could have been lifted from *The Arabian Nights*. The massive sand-colored building, with its arches and dome, looked like a mixture of mosque and Kasbah (fortress). The ballroom inside reminded me of a Moorish palace. Detail after architectural detail was, in some ways, a tribute to the Moorish and Turkish traditions that inspired the birth of the Ancient Arabic Order of the Nobles of the Mystic Shrine, better known as Shriners. I took a few pictures, but the scene, like that of a huge Disney production, was on such a colossal scale that it was hard to capture.

One can come across an almost perfect specimen of Moorish architecture in totally unexpected places, as I did when I was visiting

Cape Girardeau in southeast Missouri, a college town better known for being the birthplace of the radio talk-show host Rush Limbaugh. There, on the road running by the Mississippi river, stood a small structure, built in the 1930s, that, at first, looked like any typical mosque. It turned out to be a synagogue for the local Jewish community. The local Jews' architectural choice was no Oriental fantasy, since they themselves were often considered to be Semites from the East. As with the Moorish Revival design of the Isaac M. Wise Temple in Cincinnati, Ohio, the Central Synagogue in Manhattan, the design of the B'nai Israel Synagogue of Cape Girardeau was a conscious choice because a number of European Jews in the nineteenth century had decided that the closest style they could think of to replicate their destroyed temple in Jerusalem is a Muslim or Moorish one. In this fashion, which may strike us as ironic today, Islamic culture in America was transmitted by immigrant Jews.

Architectural landmarks, like the first Madison Square Garden (which was demolished in 1925), the New York City Center (initially named the Mecca Temple), and the fated World Trade Center in New York City, were also inspired by Moorish architecture or Islamic motifs. For Minoru Yamasaki (1912–1986), the architect who was commissioned to design the World Trade Center with its twin towers, the most favorite buildings in the world at that time (late 1950s, early 1960s) included Iran's Shah Mosque in Isfahan and the Taj Mahal in India, both built by Muslims.[19] The Twin Towers targeted by Muslim terrorists on September 11, 2001 as the ultimate emblem of American evil were, ironically, the work of a man inspired by Islamic architecture. In their typical ignorance, Islamic extremists not only targeted one of the most visible architectural legacies of Islam in America, but they also killed dozens of Muslims who were in the buildings (the estimated numbers have ranged from sixty to 358).

The Arabian Nights also exerted a good deal influence on the American imagination, including on architectural design. In the 1920s, the aviation pioneer and developer Glen Curtiss was so inspired by those tales that he tried to conjure up the city of Baghdad in Opa-Locka, north of Miami. Known as the "Baghdad of the South," Opa-Locka, according to Jonathan Curiel, "boasts of having the largest collection of 'Moorish' architecture in the Western Hemisphere. Twenty of its buildings are on the National Register of Historic Places. Streets in Opa-Locka include Ali Baba Avenue and Sharazad Boulevard."[20]

When the Masonic order of the Shriners was founded in 1872, its members, inspired by Moroccan and Turkish styles, adopted the fez and prayed in the first temple named Mecca. Echoing the language of Islam, they sought "to promote justice and suppress wrong." When new members were initiated, they had to recite an "Obligation" that states, in part, "I do hereby, upon the Bible, and on the mysterious legend of the Koran, and its dedication to the Mohammedan faith, promise and swear and vow on the faith and honor of an upright man, . . . that I will never reveal any secret part or portion of the ceremonies I have received."[21]

By 1900, more than fifty thousand Americans were members. That year, during the May parade in Washington, D.C., they greeted US President McKinley with *"salam aleikum."* In 1921, on the same occasion, US President Warren G. Harding actually responded with his own greeting of *"wa aleikum salaam."* By 1923, the president of the United States and the country's top military officer, General John Pershing, among other prominent Americans, were members. Harry Truman would also be "a devout Shriner." Over the years, the full dress regalia was toned down and even eliminated, but the fez has remained. Four hundred thousand strong today, their members include Kris Kristofferson, among other celebrities.

It really doesn't take long to come across some vestige of Muslim or Arab culture in the United States. It was during the 1904 World Fair in St. Louis that Abe Doumar turned the "flat, gridlike" Syrian pastry known as the *zalabia* into a cone that contains ice cream. For the first time in history, ice cream became portable. Coffee, one of America's most popular beverages, had come to Europe and America courtesy of Muslims. When it did, it displaced beer as a breakfast beverage in the American colonies.[22] It's hard to imagine what our recreational beverage or ice cream experiences would be without such contributions.

Coffee and ice cream are the tip of the iceberg. The United States itself, which, in the beginning was an extension of Europe and Africa, incorporated Islamic contributions, whether of Arabic origin or not, into its cultural fabric. Christopher Columbus, the ardent crusader against Islam, was given the title of *Almirante del Mar Oceano* (based on the Arabic emir, or prince, or leader). He was influenced by the ninth-century Muslim astronomer Abu-al-Abbas Ahmad al-Farghani, known as Alfraganus, who attempted to measure the Earth's diameter. "I found myself in agreement with Alfraganus," wrote Columbus. The

Italian navigator also studied the work of Abu Abdullah Mohammed al-Idrissi, author of *Al-Kitab al-Rujari* (The Book of Roger), written between 1145 and 1153 in Palermo, the first comprehensive mapping of the world sponsored by the Sicilian king, Roger II. The caravels Columbus used were named after the Arabic *qarib*. And the Spanish culture that preceded the English one in the American continent was heavily influenced by its Islamic or Moorish legacy. The linguistic and architectural traces of this legacy are still evident in the historically Spanish or Mexican parts of the United States. Words such as "alchemy," "alcohol," "algebra," "chess," "lemon," "magazine," and "zenith" are all corruptions of Arabic.[23]

To the extent that the United States is a cultural extension of Europe, it, too, benefited from the Islamic contributions that allowed Europe to develop its own civilization. Arabic was the lingua franca of scholarship in the early Middle Ages and remained so for centuries. When the twelfth-century English scholar Adelard of Bath, from England's West Country, journeyed to Antioch (present-day Antakya in Turkey), the city was teeming with religions, ethnicities, and languages, although Arabic was the predominant idiom. The Englishman was seeking the *studia Arabum*, or "the learning of the Arabs." He was, in fact, in search of the scientific and philosophical knowledge that would propel Christian Europe to a new age of discovery.[24]

The Crusades had brought Europe, with its fanatical and sometimes brutally violent hordes, to the doorsteps to the far more civilized Middle East, horrifying scholars like the Arab geographer Al-Masudi, who believed that Europeans who lived north of the Mediterranean basin were made constitutionally weak by the lack of sun and warmth in their climate. But the Crusades, as happens with many wars and clashes, civilized Europeans and introduced them to the world of global trade. Terms such as "check," "tariff," "traffic," and "arsenal" made their way into European idioms. By the time Adelard arrived in Antioch around 1114, Arab culture (which meant knowledge written and discussed in Arabic) was flourishing. People in Muslim-majority lands had discovered the astrolabe, the abacus, astronomy, mathematics (a "dangerous Saracen magic," in the words of one William of Malmesbury), and the Hindu-Arabic numeral system, which Adelard would introduce to Europe.[25]

Muslims were able to achieve so much because theology was kept in its place and did not intrude on the realm of philosophy. By breaking away from the tribal focus of the Umayyads, the first Muslim dynasty after the death of Prophet Mohammed in 632, the Abbasids started out on an extremely promising note, incorporating non-Arabs, particularly Persians, into the Islamic fold, and allowed multiple religions, cultures, and traditions to flourish in their vast empire. Such openness to diversity—which went against narrow ethnic Arab loyalties—may have made the search for foreign knowledge natural and desirable. Thus, the Abbasid caliph Abu Jafar al-Mansur conceived and built what would become the epicenter of the great Abbasid Empire, Madinat as-Salam, or Baghdad, completed around 765. Scholarship, enhanced by the importation of paper from China and an active papermaking industry, was given official support. Persian, Hindu, and Greek knowledge were highly prized, and soon a massive translation operation was underway to bring the knowledge of non-Arabic-speaking peoples to Baghdad. The institution responsible for much of this activity was *Bayt al-Hikma*, or House of Wisdom, whose mission consisted of "the safeguarding of invaluable knowledge."[26] Aristotelian ideas, though seemingly clashing with religious orthodoxy, were much admired, as were the philosophies of the Hindu sages and Persian astrologers. Islam was elevated to new levels, but so did decadence, the inevitable companion of prosperity. The Muslims' liberal borrowing from neighboring civilizations was a major advantage, allowing them to lead the way in philosophy and the sciences. Many Muslims were suspicious of religious fundamentalism and justified their contempt for Christianity, often embodied to them in the Byzantine Eastern Orthodox Church, for its rejection of Greek philosophy.

Adelard luxuriated in Arab learning. So advanced were the Arabs in scientific work and chemistry (alchemy) that they wanted to invent the elixir, a fifth essence, or quintessence—an addition to the classical Greek schema of the four elements. Here the Englishman discovered Euclid's *Elements*, "one of the greatest scientific works in history,"[27] already digested and modified by Arabs. Wary of Europe's response to his advanced secular views, Adelard hid behind the Arabs: "No one should think I am doing this out of my own head but that I am giving the views of the studies of the Arabs . . . For I know what those who profess the truth suffer at the hands of the vulgar crows. Therefore, I shall defend the cause of the Arabs, not my own." The Arabs, he said, were his "masters."[28]

Latin scholars rushed in pursuit of the *studia Arabum*, often in Spain, translating, commenting, and exporting the Arabs' refined knowledge in medicine, agriculture, cuisine, music, and literature back to emerging universities across Europe. According to the ninth-century Christian author Paul Alvarus, Arab literature was the fashion among Christian youth:

> The Christians love to read the poems and romances of the Arabs; they study the Arab theologians and philosophers, not to refute them but to form a correct and elegant Arabic. Where is the layman who now reads the Latin commentaries on the Holy Scriptures, or who studies the Gospels, prophets or Apostles? Alas! All talented Christians read and study with enthusiasm the Arab books; they gather immense libraries at great expense; they despise the Christian literature as unworthy of their attention. They have forgotten their language. For everyone who can write a letter in Latin to a friend, there are a thousand who can express themselves in Arabic with elegance, and write better poems in this language than the Arabs themselves.[29]

Ironically, it was through such knowledge that the Holy Roman Emperor Frederick II, grandson of Roger II, an inveterate and unapologetic admirer of Arab science and philosophy, was able to reclaim Jerusalem from the Ayyubid sultan Al-Kamil in 1229. His overt display of Arabic knowledge and skillful negotiations won over the sultan. Frederick II's method was a far cry from earlier crusades, particularly the first one. He sponsored translations, including of the great physician and philosopher Ibn Sina—known in the West as Avicenna (980–1037)—and the twelfth-century Aristotelian philosopher, Ibn Rushd—known in the West as Averroes—and sent copies to select universities. Thomas Aquinas studied at Frederick II's university in Naples before he joined the Dominican order and eventually adopted the Aristotelian/Averroist separation of faith and reason as the best way to protect the Christian faith. Muslims, meanwhile, in one of the greatest blunders in history, banished Averroes's work.

We cannot think about the history of African Americans without, at the same time, thinking of Islam. The first American Muslim I knew was black. I am referring to the legendary boxer Muhammad Ali, whose fights I was able to watch when I was still a child in Morocco. When I came to the United States years later, I got to hear or see other prominent African American athletes who were also Muslim. When I first looked into this phenomenon, I learned that about 7 or 8 percent of African slaves who ended up in the United

States were Muslim. The musical ways these slaves brought with them eventually gave rise to the blues, which in turn influenced other musical genres and popular bands. The memory of Islam remained remarkably alive among Americans of African descent, as they continued to convert to Islam over the centuries and decades, even when they invented hybrid theologies, as did the adherents of the Moorish Science Temple of America and the even more controversial Nation of Islam. By resisting Eurocentric domination, they found refuge in an Islam that, much like what the Shriners had done, was a blend of imagination and history adapted to their local situation. This long history of resistance played a role in the 1960s and continues to inspire young African American Muslims, including politicians and singers, to challenge their minority status.

Keith Ellison, one of these African American Muslims, a lawyer, activist, and politician from Minneapolis, established a new landmark in US politics when he was elected to the US House of Representatives in 2006. This was the first time ever in American history that a Muslim had been elected to Congress. A year later he cosponsored a Congressional resolution, introduced by Rep. Eddie Johnson from Texas, recognizing the start of the Muslim holy month of Ramadan. The following year, he was joined by thirty-three-year-old Andre Carson, a white Democrat who, like Ellison, is a convert to Islam. After Carson's election, Ellison called on American Muslims to be more conscious of their Americanness and to get more politically engaged:

> It is time we assume our place at the table . . . However defined we are by our religion, we are equally defined by our nationalism; we are Americans. As Americans, we share the pride and suffer the sorrows of all Americans. We grieved with the nation on 9/11, and we cheered with many Americans at the election of Barack Hussein Obama as president.
>
> We must become participatory citizens in the American experiment. I want to see our community give back to their country—not make the mistake that so many insular and immigrant communities make. I want to see many more Muslims serving in the U.S. Congress—instead of the two that are there now. I want to see hundreds of thousands of teachers who "happen" to be Muslim. There should be senators and mayors, state legislators, and city council members who "happen" to be Muslim. And each of you should wear a hijab or jilbab is you so choose; pray when you pray—and have it perceived as a demonstra-

tion of your faith, and not a threat to your country. I want to see and America that embraces our faith as its own—if we step out of the shadows.[30]

Literature, music, and popular culture are all inflected by Arab or Muslim influences. Khalil Gibran's *The Prophet* (1923) was a lifelong inspiration for Elvis Presley. He carried the book of Middle Eastern wisdom with him since 1956 and it remained by his side until he died in 1977. Johnny Cash, Jimmy Carter, and General Norman Schwarzkopf were all devoted to the Arab American writer who, like Elvis, deteriorated fast and succumbed to early death. Boston has had a "Khalil Gibran Day" since 2004.[31]

Fashion, too, is increasingly inspired by Moorish and Islamic motifs. The designer Karl Lagerfeld, explaining the Islamic inspiration behind his design of ankle-length skirts, said that once "cannot escape this kind of influence. It also has something mysterious, a mood of danger, something exciting."[32] In 2010, Moroccan fashion, oils, and products were all the rage, especially after the release of the blockbuster *Sex and the City 2*, which was filmed in socially liberal Morocco, not in prudish but ostentatious Abu Dhabi where the action is supposed to take place.

This fascination could be extended to poetry. Readers may be surprised to learn that the bestselling poet in the United States hails not from California or New Mexico, but from what is now northern Afghanistan. The poetry of the thirteenth-century Persian-speaking Muslim, Mawlana Jalal-al-Din Mohammed ibn Mohammed al-Balkhi—better known as Rumi—occupies a prominent place in the literature of self-help books. The poet who preached love, unity, and sweetness has been featured in "spiritual aerobics" and claimed by the gay community; his legacy is visible in the halls of "haute couture" and in the music of Philip Glass. Activists like Vanessa Redgrave rely on his Mevlevi order to preach tolerance; conservative commentators from the *National Review*, upon knowing about him, decide that Islam is not all bad; civil society activists in Iran find sustenance in his views, while Iranians—fellow Persian speakers—are bemused by Turkey's attempt to claim him for itself.[33]

This is not to talk about Muslims living right now in the United States and who are doing great by any social standard. Senegalese immigrants are transforming Harlem into bustling business districts while Los Angles boasts the largest concentration of Iranians outside

Iran. Iranian entrepreneurs span the entire spectrum of American life and business; they even own the temple of American consumerism, the Mall of America in Minnesota.[34] Muslim comedians like Aziz Ansari, entrepreneurs like Salman Khan, or journalists like Fareed Zakaria (to cite only a fraction of prominent Muslims in America) have grown into household names and faces. Even as we continue to hear about homegrown terrorist cells, and despite the public's negative views of Islam, the latter is growing at a steady pace and is bound to transform American society in the same ways that Europeans or other immigrant groups have historically changed the fabric of this nation.

What the United States and Muslim-majority nations, as well as all Muslims throughout the globe, need to do—if not enjoy a good drink, as Mark Twain mischievously suggested in his travel account, *Innocents Abroad* (1868)[35]—is find this balance in their mutual dealings. If Americans set out to change the world in their own image and trampled over the natives' rights, they also left a lasting legacy behind them that strengthened Muslims and Arabs. And if Islam appears as a threat to America and a nefarious influence on the people of Muslim-majority nations, Americans need to know that without Islam neither America nor the West would exist in the shape they do now. Through centuries of peaceful and violent contact neither side can make a claim to cultural purity. Anyone reading this book has been shaped, in various measures, by both Islam and America. Understanding this may help temper our chauvinism and reach out to one another more confidently.

Chapter 4

America's Gifts to Muslims and Arabs

American missionaries may not have been able to crack the Muslim nut, as many had expected to when they sallied forth from their new republic, armed with faith in their Protestant religions and the supremacy of their republic, but they could be forgiven for their enthusiasm because history seemed to be on their side. As fired up as they were with anti-Islamic zeal, they did a lot for Arabs, Muslims, and the Middle East, even when they failed to reach their traditional missionary objectives. At some point, the brave missionaries—and brave they were, for they were stalked by disease and death every step of the way—realized that they had to make a choice. Either they were dedicated to improving the lives of the people in the region, regardless of their conversion, or they weren't. They bet on the social mission and, in the process, changed Arabs and Muslims of the Middle East, and sometimes beyond, in profound ways.

I do not condone missionary activity of any kind as it often betrays cultural arrogance and intolerance for other people's native beliefs and traditions. It is, therefore, no wonder that the vast majority Muslims and Arabs rejected the American missionaries' attempts at their conversion. Yet, paradoxically, at no other time were Americans more admired in the Middle East and North Africa; in fact, the United States was so revered at the turn of the twentieth century that Arab immigrants to the United States became apostles of American values. This legacy is often obscured by modern grievances, but it ought to be recovered for a better understanding of America's role in empowering Arabs and Muslims.

As early as the 1830s, a missionary named Josiah Brewer asked if "the sword should not open a door . . . to the Christian preacher in Mahometan lands, may we not hope that the gradual progress of civilization will?"[1] The answer was a cautious "yes" in the beginning. Providing medical care and other social services in remote areas had a much bigger impact on native populations. Such work coincided with the great age of Manifest Destiny, a misnomer of sorts, since Americans had always been seized by the sentiment of their providential mission. By the early decades of the nineteenth century, spiritual salvation merged with Americanization. "The destiny of America inevitably bound up with the destiny of the world," declared the head of the Mosul mission.[2] The gospel of Jefferson was as strong, and, in many ways, more enduring that that of Jesus.

America, in the nineteenth century, was admired for its revolutionary past. It was considered a great and civilized nation by the Egyptian educator and reformer, Shaykh Rifa'a Rafi' al-Tahtawi (1801–1873), one that helped the region in "innumerable ways."[3] Americans were also sympathetic to Islam and its legacy. America's most famous writer in the 1820s, Washington Irving, extolled the grandeur of Islamic Spain and wrote a biography of Mohammed. Egypt, the Levant, and Turkey continued to attract visitors, although travel to such places was expensive and time consuming. To be sure, many visitors continued to deplore Islamic fanaticism and shudder at political tyranny and the treatment of religious minorities. Some even dreamed of an international crusade to end despotism and introduce Western civilization. John Lloyd Stephens—who later gained fame for exploring the Maya region in Central America—was disappointed by the ruins and dirt. Yet sordid accounts of the region sold well and did nothing to stem the enthusiasm for travel. In Mark Twain's account of his tour aboard *Quaker City* in *Innocents Abroad*, Palestine was a mere "dreamland," not a place of substance. But his account was nevertheless a bestseller and launched his successful career. The environmental deterioration of the Middle East even inspired one American ambassador in Turkey to start the Smithsonian. On the day he died, Abraham Lincoln, like many of his fellow citizens, was dreaming of visiting the Holy Land.[4]

Egypt benefited from the American Civil War: the price of cotton, a major staple of the South's economy, skyrocketed because of the American war. The North African country, which had imported a cotton gin from the United States and used American expertise in the cultivation of the crop, was encouraged to grow more to maintain the Union's economic blockade of the South and, at the same time, supply European textile mills. This newfound prosperity may have inspired the thirty-two-year-old ruler of Egypt, Khedive Ismail, who was seeking independence from Turkey and its European sponsors, to purchase US arms and recruit Civil War officers, from both sides, at the end of the war.[5]

In 1869, the year the Suez Canal was to open, Khedive Ismail asked Thaddeus Mott, colonel of a New York cavalry regiment during the Civil War and a wandering defender of freedom whom he had met a year before in Constantinople, to establish a modern army for his country. (Americans had already rebuilt the Ottoman navy following its defeat at the Battle of Navarino in 1827, and trained the Turks in naval sciences.) Within short order, Mott Pasha (as he became known locally) recruited dozens on Civil War officers from both sides of the American Civil War. The army was to be led by West Point graduate and veteran of the Mexican War, General Charles P. Stone, who proceeded to instill discipline, promote the literacy of soldiers and their children, map the topography of a country "the size of western Europe," teach geology, decide on matters as diverse as agriculture and canal construction, and expand Egyptian territory deep into the African continent. General Stone wanted to inculcate a sense of patriotism and create the foundation of Egypt's modern army. No wonder America was seen as the best friend of Muslims and Arabs. For Egyptians who aspired to progress, America, wrote the historian James Field, was "the outstanding example of a successfully developed backward country." Indeed, Khedive Tawfiq, who had taken the place of the deposed Ismail in 1879, wanted to model Egypt on the United States.[6]

Although Egypt's economic boom turned out to be short-lived, Khedive Ismail, who was admired by the American officers, dragged his country on outlandish projects that led to growing debt. By 1873, Egypt had a modern army, but the country, close to economic collapse, could no longer afford to pay the American Civil War veterans and so the Americans left the country for new prospects.[7]

The year the American Civil War ended marked the birth of the first major American college in a Muslim land—Robert College in Turkey. Two American men—the schoolmaster and nonconformist Cyrus Hamlin and the wealthy philanthropist Christopher Robert— wanted to introduce American-style education to the Middle East and were granted a charter the following year by the Board of Regents of the State of New York. Older than the Massachusetts Institute of Technology and the University of California, Robert College reflected the American spirit at its best and proved the value of cultural diplomacy. It was the only institution allowed to fly a foreign flag above the Bosporus until 1971. Gilbert and Edwin Grosvenor, the two editors who established the *National Geographic* magazine, spent time on the campus when their father was teaching there. Turkey and the United States avoided war because of the mediation of the alumni of this college.[8]

Inspired by the success of his project, Hamlin proposed an even more daring idea: a college for girls. In 1890, the Commonwealth of Massachusetts granted The American College for Girls a charter allowing it to confer the degree of Bachelor of Arts. This was the college that graduated the first female associate of Kemal Ataturk, the founder of modern Turkey. Robert College, meanwhile, would graduate some of the most prominent leaders of the nation. It is not for no reason that Robert College is said to have inspired a new Turkish nationalism. When Hamlin's two colleges merged to concentrate on secondary education in the 1970s, Turkey set up Bogaziçi University on Robert's old grounds.[9]

Around the same time Hamlin was trying to set up a college in Turkey, the missionary Daniel Bliss was pursuing the same goal in Lebanon. After raising money in the United States and England and obtaining a charter from the State of New York, he opened the Syrian Protestant College in late 1866. The college was decidedly Protestant, but Bliss accepted anyone who applied and qualified. "A man white, black, or yellow; Christian, Jew, Mohammedan or heathen," he wrote years later, "may enter and enjoy all the advantages of the institution for three, four or eight years; and go out believing in one God, in many Gods, or in no God." In 1920, following political map redrawings of the region (Maronite-denominated Lebanon having been carved out by the French from the larger Syria), the name was changed to the American University of Beirut.[10]

By 1870, the Middle East was peppered with schools, churches, or clinics founded and run by Americans. Notions of patriotism, republicanism, and human rights were introduced through these secular institutions, eventually leading Arabs to imagine themselves as a separate nation, a "new Phoenicia, a new Syria,"[11] in the words of the missionary Henry Jessup. Even when Britain started its seventy-two-year occupation of Egypt in 1882 and all Western powers were caught up in the fever of imperialism and theories of racial supremacy, American missionaries carried on with their secular mission. And their success was staggering. By 1885, they had invested close to a million dollars in education and publishing, ran eight colleges, seventy-five secondary schools, and hundreds of elementary schools in the Ottoman provinces.[12] And there was more, as Michael Oren describes:

> In the single decade between 1885 and 1895, the budget for missionary institutions in the Middle East expanded sevenfold. In addition to over four hundred schools and nine colleges with a total enrollment of 20,000, the money also paid for nine hospitals and ten dispensaries treating an estimated 40,000 patients annually. Along with journals, newspapers, and Bibles in five Middle Eastern languages, American presses rolled out some four million textbooks on topics ranging from astronomy to dentistry, lithography to moral philosophy.[13]

Arabs and Muslims were certainly grateful for the amenities; but unlike in the Far East, they refused to convert. To do so in Arabia was even more hopeless, as the Reformed Dutch missionary Samuel Zwemer found out after an arduous journey that eventually brought him back to Princeton where he helped establish the Department of Near Eastern Studies. Preaching the "Social Gospel" was the best American missionaries could accomplish. Some Americans, like Alexander Russell Webb, a former consul to the Philippines, went even farther than that and actually converted to Islam.[14]

Tourism continued to boom, with the typical consequences that befall host nations. Egyptian guides tried to speak English with an American accent. Monuments were vandalized or stolen. Tourists felt superior to the locals, acting like "ugly Americans," although the great African American writer, Frederick Douglass, saw Arabs as models and "half brothers to the Negro."[15] American travelers usually began in Egypt then continued on to Palestine (Jaffa and Jerusalem) before sailing to Istanbul. Major dignitaries received royal treatment, but like everybody else, they grew gradually disenchanted with the region. Ulysses S. Grant was treated as the "king of America" in Egypt when he visited in 1878, but his wife Julia expressed both their views when she commented: "Egypt, the birthplace of civilization— Egypt, the builder of temples, tombs, and the great pyramids—has nothing."[16] Grant probably enjoyed reading Mark Twain's account of his tour aboard more than he did the actual trip.[17]

Despite such misgivings about modern Egypt, Americans, like Europeans, were fascinated by the country's ancient monuments. The magnate William H. Vanderbilt asked Khedive Ismail for an obelisk for New York and was offered the famous Cleopatra's Needle, better than what any European power had gotten, as another token of gratitude to the United States. Ismail backed down when European powers objected, but when he was replaced by his son Tawfiq, the wealthy Vanderbilt covered all the necessary expenses and had the obelisk shipped to New York, where it was erected to great excitement in 1881.[18]

Ismail himself was given the opportunity by the French sculptor Frédéric Auguste Bartholdi to erect a statue, twice the height of the Sphinx, to serve as a lighthouse at the entrance of the Suez Canal that had been excavated by the Frenchman Ferdinand de Lesseps. It was to be named *Egypt (or Progress) Bringing Light to Asia*, but Khedive Ismail was broke and could not commit. So, Bartholdi, a fervent admirer of liberty and the United States, redirected his attention to another city and country. The figures and mottos changed, but that's how the 225-ton Statue of Liberty (whose foundation was built under the supervision of none other than General Stone) came to be unveiled in 1886 in the city of New York. How ironic it was, then, when the great Arab American poet Ameen Rihani later wondered why Arabs didn't have a similar symbol for liberty. "Shall the future never see a statue of freedom near the Pyramids?" Rihani lamented.[19] Little did he know that Muslims had their chance before the Americans, but they squandered it.

The United States entered the twentieth century with even more global strength and confidence, but the drive for resources, imperial misadventures, and the US government's unconditional support of the newly created state of Israel drove an ever-increasing wedge between Muslims and Americans. These new twentieth-century realities engendered a new kind of violence, that of terrorism. American leaders struck what seems like a devil's bargain deal with Saudi Arabia: the latter would allow the United States unrestricted access to its oil in return for guaranteed security. Together the two nations worked to undermine Soviet Communism and secular Arab nationalism while the United States helped the Saudis to promote their morbid brand of Islam. The result of this unholy alliance worked all right—the Soviets were eventually expelled from Afghanistan and their "evil" empire collapsed soon thereafter, while Arab nationalism was displaced by the fury of Islamic fundamentalism. International chaos ensued, as nonstate organizations, like Al-Qaeda, emerged to terrorize the world in the name of some alleged Islamic purity. The puritanical Muslims that the United States helped promote were now fighting America's meddling in Muslim nations and seeking to expel Americans from Saudi Arabia. Because the governments of Arab and Muslim nations appeared too servile to the United States and no officially sanctioned party or movement could express itself freely within these govern-ments, Muslim extremists filled the political vacuum and turned into the only credible resistance movement in the Muslim world. However, their terroristic methods helped perpetuate the traditional negative image of Islam and Arabs in American culture.

As a new century and millennium dawned, Americans and Muslims found themselves ensnared in one of the worst conflicts in their his-tory. The United States appeared like an "innocent abroad," caught up in the political and cultural machinations of old civilizations and faiths, but it was also driven by half-coherent strategic interests (such as its faithful alliance with Saudi Arabia and other autocratic regimes in the region), bombing its way to whatever political outcome it sought. I say half-coherent because it has never been clear to me how massive expenditures of resources and human lives to overthrow regimes and bomb insurgents benefit the vital interest of our country. This may not be necessarily a statement about the United States per se, because one can't expect states to behave rationally, in the sense that they would take account of all the knowledge available to us and make decisions that enhance the course of human civilization. The firepower of the United States was not preventing the country from growing more vulnerable on the world stage; the more it resorted to using force, the more it was perceived as somewhat weakened, including by nations who show it proper deference. Our age's only superpower, addicted to Middle Eastern oil and determined to keep its potential rivals, China and Russia, at bay, was trapped into wars, fights, and political skirmishes with nonstate organizations like the Taliban, terrorist organizations like Al-Qaeda, and ancient nations like Iran. It was a ruinous course, one that was compounded by the nation's equally incoherent economic and political systems. We'll talk more about this in the next chapter.

The toxic fumes of oil were not dissipating. Not only is the massive consumption of this fuel damaging our global habitat and creating a frustrating dependency inside the United States, but, until the second decade of the twenty-first century, when Tunisians, Egyptians, Libyans, and other Arabs revolted against their corrupt leaders, it had strengthened the autocratic governments of oil states and compromised America's universalist ideology of freedom. Thus, while the American public is exposed to the tales of Iranian repression and dictatorship, almost nothing is said about the conglomeration of Arab Gulf states, whose tribal—or, more accurately, apartheid—systems are as anathema as any political system can get to the American democratic model. The hypocrisy is there for anyone to see, yet it rarely registers in political pronouncements. Secretary of State Hillary Clinton did warn Arab leaders on the eve of the toppling of the Tunisia's Ben Ali's regime, but the US government, despite its support for democratic change in the region, never lent robust support to the Saudis, Bahrainis, and others seeking radical reform in the oil-rich sheikdoms of the Arabian Gulf.

There is also the problem of perception. Since Americans started traveling to the Holy Land, they have been disappointed by the backwardness of the region, but few ever pondered why and how great civilizations grow ruinous. Unsavory as countries like Iraq, Iran, Egypt, and the whole of the Middle East may be to some American travelers, they also gave birth to human civilization. This is where law, writing, and religion, not to mention agriculture, were first practiced. They went into decline when Europe's seaborne commerce displaced land-based trade. Even when their power dwindled and entered the modern era in a vulnerable state, Muslims had no problem with Europe and actively sought its democratic systems. But European powers colonized them instead and displayed a violent double standard that made Muslims and Arabs appreciate the United States. The Muslim-Arab relationship with the United States began to change only during the middle of the twentieth century, as the United States pursued objectives that seemed almost antithetical to what the self-sacrificing missionaries in the nineteenth century tried to accomplish.

The image of crazed religious extremists or disheveled terrorists shouldn't lead us to believe that the whole region is teeming with such folk or that European civilization is on the verge of being overtaken by Muslim fanatics. Countries like Egypt may take pride in their Muslim heritage, but they also care about their tourist industry. The Muslims I know enjoy Western freedoms, and few would contemplate living in oil-rich but socially restrictive Arab nations. Moroccans, for example, were openly challenging the conservatives mores of their nation—breaking the fast publicly as a sign of protest against laws criminalizing eating-while-Muslim in public during the month of Ramadan, publishing gay novels and magazines, and declaring their atheism in blogs and other forums—before the outbreak of the Arab Spring in 2011. Morocco tends to be socially liberal, perhaps because it has no oil or natural gas. It is an agricultural society with an increasingly diversified economy in technology sectors, aviation, and other fields, which makes its people more self-reliant and entrepreneurial than members of oil-rich economies. I once met a Moroccan man and his Lebanese colleague in a forum sponsored by an oil-rich Arab state and asked them what they were doing there. They mischievously told me that they had been invited because of their brainpower, not the size of their wallets. Gulf states may want to switch to solar energy and plan for a nonoil economy, but living off natural resources, whether it is the sun or oil, through the help of foreign know how is not a mark of progress.

Today, as we make further inroads into the twenty-first-century, all Muslim-majority nations, from West Africa to East Asia, can still learn from the dedication of a group of American missionaries in the middle of the nineteenth century. Muslims have yet to create institutions of higher learning that come close to matching Bogaziçi University in Istanbul (the successor to Robert College), the American University of Beirut, or the American University of Cairo. Gulf states in the Arabian Peninsula are pouring billions of dollars into building monumental campuses, brand-name museums, and even cities dedicated to science, research, and medicine; but they are doing so in the same way they are building new islands, fancy hotels, malls, and ice rinks. The engineering and planning are, again, being done by educated Westerners or by Western-educated Arabs Muslims, while the backbreaking labor falls on the shoulders of poor Asians and other desperate immigrants. These wealthy Muslims, whose resources were discovered and exploited for them by Westerners, are merely consumers of American or Western modernity. They may be savvy bankers and real estate investors, grabbing up landmarks hotels and buildings in New York and London, but such money games are not the essence of progress and development. Even when the United States was waging a war against the Taliban in Afghanistan, its geologists and military officers helped discover huge amounts of mineral deposits—things like iron, copper, cobalt, gold, and lithium—that could utterly transform the economy of that desolate country. Once again, as happened before with Saudi Arabia, the reviled American infidel was bringing news of wealth to long-suffering Muslims.

This is not to say that the United States has not had a negative impact of Muslims and Arabs. Its political machinations and military interventions have caused real injury to the people of the Middle East and North Africa. Still, without colonizing the region, Americans gave much to Arabs and Muslims. They planted the seed for Arab revivalism and nationalism when they educated Arab students by using Arabic fonts and presses they imported with them. The early Arab converts to Protestantism called themselves "nationals," or "*watani-yyun*," and the graduates of their schools, empowered by their modern education, thought of themselves as part of larger groups of Arabs. One of the most prominent of these converts and graduates, Butrus al-Bustani (1819–1883), turned into a veritable Renaissance man, publishing encyclopedias and journals, opening a National School in Beirut, and advocating the separation of state and church. By the first decade of the twentieth century, American missionaries were running "975 primary and secondary schools and 15 colleges, educating 64,000 students in all grades. They also administered 49 hospitals and 63 dispensaries that cared for over 650,000 patients."[20]

Not only that, penniless Arabs and Muslims actually immigrated to America and, as I indicated in the introduction, flourished in a way that is unprecedented anywhere in the world. Between 1880 and 1914, the statue that Bartholdi built welcomed one hundred thousand Syrians or so—Arabs of present-day nations Syria, Lebanon, Jordan, Israel, and the Palestinian Authority—the same way it did Italians and other Europeans. Many started out peddling dry goods and other items, and although they have endured a fair amount of racial or ethnic discrimination, they enriched their new nation with major contributions in all fields.[21] They published Arabic newspapers and played an important role in the formation of Arab nationalism. Because they were forced to transcend narrow religious identification and become one community identified by its language and race, they were able to see all Levantines as Arabs, not just Maronite, Greek Orthodox, or Muslim, as they had been accustomed to do.

It may well be that the Syrians' common experience in the *mahjar* (lands of immigration) helped make of them a nation in the modern sense. Because of the Ottoman Empire's alliance with the Central Powers during World War I, and then the Ottoman policy of Turkification, many Syrians in the United States, already conscious of their new identity, distanced themselves from the Ottomans and took up the case of independence. Unlike the smaller group of Arabists who wanted to remain within Ottoman sovereignty, these Syrians saw their glorious Arab civilization as constrained by Ottoman rule. Arabs, they were convinced, could still do great things, as exemplified by their own experience in the West.[22]

Now is the time to reflect a bit about how a few Arabs and Muslims viewed the United States in the course of the twentieth century. (I will add my own impressions later in this chapter.) The most infamous Muslim visitor (and brief resident) of this country must surely be now Sayyid Qutb (1906–1966), the intellectual guide to many a Muslim extremist today, a literary critic who joined the Egyptian Muslim Brothers and turned political activist before he was imprisoned and executed by President Nasser, the Arab nationalist American politicians deplored, in 1966. In 1948, the Egyptian government sent him to the United States to learn more about pedagogy. Unlike the Syrians who had arrived in America earlier in the century, Qutb was not culturally prepared to adapt to American society and may very well have been traumatized by the whole experience.

Upon his return to Egypt in 1950, he wrote an essay titled "The America I Have Seen" (1951). The land and the people are spellbindingly beautiful, he acknowledged; its people are highly productive. But Americans remain "abysmally primitive in the world of the senses, feeling, and behavior." They are unnaturally violent and favor applied science because it allows them to build and conquer. They are given to "sheer physical gratification" and are impressed by numbers. They attend church but are not pious. They are stressed despite their abundant material life. Their art revolves around simplistic plots. These are people of low moral values, and their jazz is nothing more than the "music that the savage bushmen created to satisfy their primitive desires, and the desire for noise on the one hand, and the abundance of animal noises on the other."[23]

Qutb's essay must count as one of the most damning verdicts of the United States by a Muslim or Arab traveler, but it may also reflect his deep disappointment at the US recognition and support of Israel, which happened while he was visiting. Many other travelers had a more nuanced or even charmingly naïve view of the country, including Bartholdi, the maker of Statue of Liberty, who also found Americans difficult to like. But most Arabs marveled at the American work ethic, which was unknown in the Arab world, as it is still today. When Philip K. Hitti, the academic of Syrian-Lebanese background who taught at Princeton and authored the well-known *History of the Arabs*, published his account of life in America in 1924, he expressed wonder at the differences between Americans and Arabs on the question of work. But he attributed these propensities to American materialism, on one hand, and Eastern spirituality, on the other.

> Were the American to stand and watch the waters that separate Brooklyn from the rest of New York, he would think of building a bridge on which trains and cars can pass, carrying people from one side to another. But were the easterner to stand and watch the same waters, he would probably compose a poem.[24]

This comparative view of the two civilizations, or cultures, was shared by the Rev. Abraham Rihbany, an Arab Protestant minister in America, and author of the autobiography, *A Far Journey* (1917), who believed that East and West must remain separate in their essences because each embodies a natural indispensable virtue. If the West is materialistic and business driven, the East is spiritually and poetically inclined.

But Ameen Rihani (1876–1940), the first Arab American writer to explore the differences and ways to bridge them in both English and Arabic, disagreed with such sharp polarities. Arriving in the United States in 1888 at the tender age of twelve, Rihani was able to acquire a most cosmopolitan education and distance himself from narrow ethnic and religious loyalties, including his own Maronite church. He was influenced by the work of American Transcendentalists and the poetry of Walt Whitman, as well as by the poetry of the great Arab skeptic, Abul 'Ala' al-Ma'arri (974–1058), whose work he translated. In a poem titled "A Chant of Mystics" (1921), the position of Rihani was as clear as could be:

Nor Crescent nor Cross we adore;
Nor Budha nor Christ we implore;
Nor Muslem nor Jew we abhor:
  We are free.

We are not of Iran or of Ind,
We are not of Arabia or of Sind:
 We are free.
We are not of the East of the West;
No boundaries exist in our breast:
 We are free.[25]

This is, in my opinion, a far more civilized approach to the modern
world than the narrow, polarizing views later espoused by Qutb and
that still afflict many Muslims to this day. To be sure, Rihani knew
that Europe was a bullying power. At one point, he even suspected
the Europeans of encouraging religious fanaticism among Arabs so
as to keep them in fetters. The European Dragon, "which is fed by
the foreign missionary and the ulema [Muslim theologians], and
which still preys upon the heart and mind of the Orient nations, is
as active to-day as it was ten centuries ago," he wrote in 1918.[26] Nor
was Rihani oblivious to the kind of excessive American materialism noted by other Arab or Muslim visitors. In *The Book of Khalid*
(1911), the first Arab American novel ever written, the protagonist,
while in prison, sorts out the dual impressions of America on his
mind—the crude pursuit of materialism and the promise of freedom.
Although Americans are "honest votaries of Mammon," he has faith
that the time will come when they will outgrow this fetish and reach
for their better angels. Then the promise of his beloved America will
shine in all its glory:

To these United States shall the Nations of the World turn one day for
the best model of good Government; in these United States the well-
springs of the higher aspirations of the soul shall quench the thirst of
every race-traveler on the highway of emancipation; and from these
United States the sun and moon of a great Faith and a great Art shall
rise upon mankind.

Speaking through his protagonist, and echoing Emerson and Whitman, Khalid envisions the day when the American Superman shall
rise in the New World and the United States will assume its "world-
ruling destiny."

From his transcendental height, the Superman of America shall ray
forth in every direction the divine light, which shall mellow and purify
the spirit of Nations and strengthen and sweeten the spirit of men, in

this New World, I tell you, he shall be born, but he shall not be an American in the Democratic sense. He shall be nor of the Old World nor of the New; he shall be, my Brothers, of both. In him shall be reincarnated the Asiatic spirit of origination, of Poesy and Prophecy, and the European spirit of Art, and the American spirit of Invention. Ay, the Nation that leads the world to-day in material progress shall lead it, too, in the future, in the higher things of the mind and soul.[27]

The nationalist Rihani placed his hope in his adopted nation's support for the independence of Arabs from the Ottoman Empire and even dreamed of a United Arab States based on the American experience. He was as grateful to America, as the Rev. Rihbany had been, when he wrote: "So to Syria, my loving, untutored mother, as to America, my virile, resourceful teacher, I offer my profound and lasting gratitude."[28] Contemplating the Middle East toward the end of World War I, Rev. Rihbany actually called on the "free and large-hearted America" to lead the world and provide protection to his native Syria as it tried to forge its path toward the future and emulate America's well-tried federal system. He pleaded with America that it was morally and constitutionally bound to help the cause of freedom and progress, and that it should now "go east" and help his fellow Syrians work out a system of government that would leave Syria whole and not divided into sectarian mini-states. For this reason, he disagreed with the long-term Zionist plan of extricating Palestine from larger Syria. (He was equally opposed to an independent Lebanon, although he was born near Mount Lebanon.)[29]

In fact, no less a figure than George Antonius, the father of Arab nationalism, in his classic, *The Arab Awakening*, acknowledged France and the United States as "foster-parents of the Arab resurrection."[30] The greatness and uniqueness of the United States were celebrated even by people who developed a dim view of the nation. When France and Britain started dividing Syria after the World War I, many Syrians yearned to return back to help, including the physician Michael Shadid, the visionary who introduced cooperative health care to the United States.

Dr. Shadid's first taste of freedom and opportunity occurred when his family moved from a small village on the slope of Mount Lebanon to Beirut, where he was able to attend the American university founded by the missionary Daniel Bliss. He spent the "three happiest years" of his life enjoying the "free and democratic spirit" that reigned at that American campus. To him, the American University of Beirut was "a potent form for enlightenment" in a city and country filled with religious bigotry and intolerance. Thirty years after he immigrated to the United States, and after a successful career in medicine, he tried to return and give back to his native land, only to find out that his birthplace was as primitive as he had left it (with, once again, the notable exception of the American institution). He then knew that the United States was the only country he could call home. "Yes," he wrote, "home was the right word. I had given up all thought of returning to Syria and decided to spend the rest of my days in the United States. We went back to Elk City [in Oklahoma], and that town has remained our home and the center of my activities to the present day."[31]

Dr. Shadid's story is recounted proudly by Salom Rizk, a fellow Arab American, in his equally moving tribute to America, *Syrian Yankee* (1943). Born an orphan in the Syrian village of Ain Arab, Rizk suffered the worst poverty and hardships, including being homeless and working as a swineherd, not knowing that he was an American citizen by birth until, at around the age of thirteen when he tried to seek an education, a school teacher found out and told him that he actually belonged to the heaven that is America. This revelation triggered an odyssey that took the boy through Beirut and five years of waiting before he finally boarded a ship to America, landed in New York, and took the train to Sioux City to be reunited with his family. Without much fluency in English, the adult Rizk shared his story with fourth-grade schoolmates, then gradually with the rest of the school and the whole nation. America, to him, was the world's last best hope.[32]

One could assume that Rev. Rihbany's, Ameen Rihani's, Dr. Michael Shadid's, and Salom Rizk's idealization of the United States, in contrast to the condemnation of Qutb, may have been motivated by their attempt to assimilate in their new homeland and avoid discrimination based on their ethnicity or skin color. Qutb had nothing to lose after he left the country, but the Syrians who came to the United States decades before his visit couldn't afford that attitude. This is not implausible since early Syrian immigrants were subject to discriminatory attitudes and laws. They even went to court to make a case for their whiteness.[33] Qutb may have suffered from similar attitudes when he visited the country, but he also seemed to know very little about his host country's history or the revolution that made it in the first place. In fact, he would have been happier visiting early

Puritans of the seventeenth century than he did the Americans of the twentieth. Perhaps because they had adopted the United States as their new home, immigrants like Rihani negotiated the tensions that result from dislocation and straddling two vastly different worlds and traditions successfully. Unlike fundamentalists of all stripes, they opted for a cosmopolitan outlook.

The conflicting views of America, both globally and even nationally, are inevitable given the size and history of the country. It is a nation of many trends and backgrounds, where the past exists in tension with the present, prosperity is threatened with collapse, secularism challenged by the ghosts of the Puritan past, and the passion for freedom at home is undermined by the drive for control abroad. The country continues to be an experiment, which is at it should be, since being alive means going through changes. But the United States is also is a nation that exerts tremendous influence on people from Muslim-majority nations, including on those, like my native city in Morocco, that are far removed from the actual Holy Land.

Like anyone growing up in the twentieth century, America was both a felt reality and a dreamlike place for me long before I ever crossed the Atlantic Ocean to land in New York. Americans didn't have as much of a presence in Morocco as they did in the Middle East—Morocco, by the Christians' book, is no Holy Land. In fact, if anything, my native city of Tangier had long been considered a free-for-all zone, a place of unregulated hedonism and free sexuality, a refuge for those Europeans or Americans hounded by the law or Puritan morality. As social mores relaxed in the West and the city's population grew somewhat more bourgeois, Western artists and bohemians stopped coming in large numbers and were replaced by another group of Puritans seeking freedom and pleasure: oil-rich Arabian sheiks.

Tangier has never been dominated by Americans in the way it has by other ancient and more modern powers. But the presence of America in Tangier is unmistakable. It was in this city that America's oldest peace and friendship treaty with any nation in the world was made visible. Two years after President Washington named James Simpson consul in 1797, the sultan of Morocco, Moulay Slimane, offered a building to his successor Consul John Mullawny for perpetual use by United States. That building has served many functions throughout the centuries that followed. It has been expanded and turned into a well-known cultural center in the old city, appropriately located in "Rue d'Amérique." It now stands as first building not located on US soil to be listed on the National Register of Historic Places. When, in the mid-1860s, the United States was invited to join a consortium of nine European nations to build a lighthouse at Cape Spartel, near a treacherous part of the ocean where the Atlantic Ocean and the Mediterranean meet, it would be the first time the nation would adhere to a multinational treaty. The US Congress appropriated money for the maintenance of the lighthouse for three-quarters of a century. The United States was so highly regarded by the Moroccan sultan around that time that, according to an account published in *Foreign Affairs* in 1945, he was willing to place his whole empire under US protectorate than allow any European power to take over.[34]

Americans also started a school in 1950 using the State of Pennsylvania's curriculum. The Woolworth heiress and benefactress, Barbara Hutton, by then a well-known resident of the city, provided the initial funding and scholarships. This school, whose headmaster was at one point was Omar Shakespeare Pound, graduated a good number of students who eventually made their way to the United States and prospered. And it was in Tangier that the impresario capitalist and publisher, Malcolm Forbes, threw his lavish seventieth birthday party in 1999 shortly before he passed away.

One of most memorable experiences for me as a child in the early 1970s was discovering the American spirit of freedom in, not surprisingly, American films. Despite all myths to the contrary, the American dream, I learned early on, is not just about making money. It is about the freedom to be oneself, to live up to one's beliefs without governmental or corporate coercion. To me, Americans were inveterate romantics (an idiosyncrasy that includes what historian Walter McDougall called hustling[35]), constantly dreaming up schemes of freedom, which may explain the tendency to violence so often decried by US liberals and foreigners alike. In fact, America sometimes strikes me as somewhat primitive, in the sense that basic human emotions still appear in their unvarnished primordial form, untouched by the pretense of refinement.

As children, when we saw groups of American tourists walking through the oldest part of town, known as the Medina or the Kasbah, we shouted things like "hello." And when we saw African Americans, we yelled "soul brother," without understanding what such expressions meant. We always got big hearty laughs from these friendly tourists. People who worked in hotels loved Americans because they were the best tippers. Americans spoke loudly, to be sure, but they didn't seem to have a care in the world. When their frigates or aircraft carriers docked outside the city, it was a bit of a sensation. When I was in high school, I took my young cousin to a US aircraft carrier and we were welcomed like important dignitaries. Even then, I knew that Americans were not bound by the deeply felt structures of hierarchy that prevail in most of the world.

The rise of a country of wild-eyed adventurers, New World enthusiasts, and sober Protestant dissidents into the most powerful empire in world history is simply a mesmerizing tale and a great story to contemplate. After all, one could reasonably assert that most people in the world are, in some ways, American. Children are often exposed to American morality tales in American-made cartoons, movies, or TV icons. I can't conceive my childhood in Tangier without the TV shows *Bonanza*; *Hawaii Five-O*; *Rich Man, Poor Man*; *Columbo*; and *The Fugitive*, among others. Although, as a Mediterranean boy, I wanted to be Hercules, Spartacus, and other heroes from the classical world, I identified more closely with the characters in spaghetti Western movies (so-called because they were made by Italians who were also fascinated by America).

To me, the quintessential American was Clint Eastwood's Man without a Name in Italian filmmaker Sergio Leone's *The Good, the Bad, and the Ugly*. A man from nowhere, without any human bonds, Blondie (as Tuco, his Mexican rival and partner, calls him), develops his own code of virtue, which, like Tuco's, can be summed up in the making of money by twisting the law to his advantage. As a bounty hunter, Blondie captures dangerous criminals, but he also uses his sharp-shooting skills to untie the knot around their necks, allowing them to flee the hanging platform and the death penalty—increasing the bounty on their heads—before he captures them again for a better reward. Poker faced, Blondie (the Good) is a man of few words who doesn't wear his heart on his sleeve, but, on occasion, as when he witnesses the mass slaughter during the Civil War and the futile death of brave commanders and young soldiers ("Never so many men who were wasted so badly," he remarks), he does offer dying victims a puff or two from his half-burnt cigar. And when he gets a hold of the two-hundred-thousand-dollar cash box in a grave, kills the unscrupulous Angel Eyes (the Bad) in a shootout, ties a rope around Tuco's neck and hands, he rides away with half the bounty only, leaving Tuco (the Ugly) the other half in the midst of a sprawling cemetery. Just before he gets out of sight for good, he looks back and, like in the old days of their partnership, shoots the rope around Tuco's neck, but leaves his hands tied.

When this movie was first released in New York City, the *New York Times* critic Renata Adler described it as so violent that anyone who remained in the theatre after one violent scene "is not someone I should care to meet, in any capacity, ever."[36] Yet, when I first saw this film as a child, I thought it was a parable of freedom and justice in a no-man's land. I have spent all my life whistling Ennio Morricone's uplifting and melancholy musical score. People may not know what to make of Blondie, but Sergio Leone saw him as the prototype of the men who opened up America's frontier—strong, self-reliant, and lonely. "The West was made by violent uncomplicated men," Leone said, "and it is this strength and simplicity that I try to recapture in my pictures."[37]

I once started writing a novel based on the retelling of *The Good, the Bad, and the Ugly* because I thought it explained much about America. My friends thought I was making excuses to indulge in one of my favorite films, but when I opened historian Walter McDougall's history of American's encounter in with the world, *Promised Land, Crusader State* (1997), in the summer of 2010, I was astonished to find that he starts his discussion of America's national traits, inherited from biblical and secular traditions, that have propelled the United States in wrongheaded crusades to make the world a better place, with a discussion of the same film. If Adler wouldn't care to meet those of us who like the film, one of the greatest historians of our age tells that all three main characters in Leon's film are actually us, meaning Americans who are "at once typically flawed human beings, unique individualists obsessed with both justice and money, and citizens of the most powerful, hence potentially the most corruptible, country on earth."[38]

The influence of American culture on a Moroccan kid was by no means a unique experience; it was, in fact, universal. Sergio Leone himself was smitten by Hollywood tales when he was nine or ten years old. "We were madly in love with American cinema," he later recalled, "always imitating Errol Flynn and Gary Cooper."[39] In 2004, the British author and journalist Polly Toynbee, after noting the decline of interest in American studies, acknowledged that despite current displeasure with US policy, "the idea of America is woven deep into the universal imagination. When prompted, the world can also admit to seeing the United States as that beacon of liberty and opportunity that Americans dream themselves to be." Then Toynbee continued:

> Hardly a child born can avoid drinking in the great American myth from those Disney realms where the simple, humble and virtuous win through every time against the rich, corrupt and greedy. How is that self-image squared with the monster the world perceives? The old Hollywood morality tales from *Shane* and *It's a Wonderful Life* still spin out into *Spiderman* or *I, Robot*, celebrating the little guy who beats the monster corporation. Homespun American goodness warring with the cruelties of raw capitalism is the dominant Hollywood theme, yet little of this culture enters the US political bloodstream.

Many years after my discovery of Blondie, I found that same spirit in New York City, where I first landed in 1983. Arriving at JFK airport was a mesmerizing experience. Immigration and customs officers checked my papers and luggage professionally and courteously, the airport businesses were customer-friendly, buses arrived on time, and, most stunningly, coffee was available "to go" in a Greek-themed blue-and-white cup stating "We Are Happy to Serve You." I felt like a strange, latter-day Pilgrim (Cotton Mather would probably be rolling in his grave) greeted by the same air of freedom that welcomed the Puritans or Tom Paine.

Less than four hundred years after the Mayflower's historic voyage, America presents a multicolored face, one that makes it easier for the immigrant to blend in, and, if one listens carefully, it also seems to speak in tongues, although English and Spanish dominate the Babelian hierarchy. Like seventeenth-century Pilgrims, most immigrants and students who arrive to America's shores are reluctant to go back to their native lands, for once they experience the freedoms and possibilities of being in America, who would want to return to a world of social limitations, bureaucratic indignities, and unfulfilling lives for the rich and poor alike? Those who are not ready to be assimilated into America's mainstream culture gravitate toward the halfway houses of ethnic enclaves, rediscover their roots, and begin to develop a complex love–hate relationship with a culture they like and fear, much like the Pilgrims' experience in Holland before they packed up and left.

It takes time to become an American, but once one acquires the cultural capital to be fully initiated into the American universe, the rest of the world appears rather puny, more like a historical or anthropological curiosity, an exotic land of diverse natural beauty, colorful people, and good cuisine—all residues of a long-surpassed world order. Even since English saints and strangers landed in the New World, America, and later its offspring, the United States, has been the land of the future, human civilization's frontier and destination. A Moroccan proverb says that entering a public bath is not the same as leaving it. One could apply a similar principle to America: once one crosses into the future, it's harder (if not impossible) to step back in time.

Probably because I studied American literature and culture in graduate school, I have often been asked to describe America, to provide a sort of alternative picture of a country that has come to be known outside America's borders almost exclusively through the sheer might of its military firepower, economic prowess, and entertainment muscle. People do know there is more to the empire than what flickers on their TV screens or is printed on the front pages of their local papers, but how does one begin to explain? If I were to say that America is the land of freedom, I would be asked about the Native Americans and people of African descent. I remember when I took a few colleagues on a tour of Morocco, a young university student in a small village near Marrakech, in one of the most beautiful and idyllic settings one could imagine, asked his American visitors rather matter-of-factly about the fate of Native Americans, almost as if the latter were his long-lost distant cousins. And of course the much-resented American popular culture has transmitted the suffering and sensibilities of the African Diaspora, leaving the strong impression that millions of transplanted people have yet to enjoy the promise of the American Revolution. After the events of 9/11, Muslims, convinced that a plot has been hatched against them and that their religion has been targeted for America's next crusade, joined the ranks of the aggrieved.

If establishing America meant disposing of the natives, enslaving Africans, indenturing Europeans, and, over time, overreaching back to the world the English settlers and revolutionaries had gladly left behind, it also meant unleashing the spirit of dissent that the brave Pilgrims brought with them, making it harder for dogmas to coalesce into eternal certitudes or regimes. Even as white Europeans were attacking Indians, others were helping them and defending their rights. Many profited from the black slave system, but others fought hard to abolish it. And although Islam was generally presented as the emblem of infidelity during the colonial period and of despotism during the revolutionary one, quite a few writers, as I have indicated, presented a balanced view of the religion, and even praised it when they thought it deserved to be defended. Thomas Jefferson, the main author of the Declaration of Independence, explicitly protected Muslims' rights in Virginia, even as his state deported Arab-looking men. And if Africans suffered untold indignities in white America and many continue to endure debilitating hardships today, white Americans have also elected a black president with a vaguely Muslim heritage.

The United States is certainly the land of opportunity, unique among the world's nations, in this regard. More than twenty years after I arrived in the United States, when I was practically living with my son in the hospital, I came across stories of resistance and survival that reminded me of the American spirit I had cherished in my childhood in Tangier. One that struck me most was about Jesse James Hardy, a jolly-looking, sixty-eight-year-old, white-bearded, skinny man with prostate cancer who turned down the state of Florida's 4.5 million-dollar offer to buy his 160-acres of scrubby and dusty land, which he had bought for only $60,000 in 1976, as part of an 8.4 billion-dollar project to restore the Everglades. He wanted to stay on his farm with his late girlfriend's niece and her sick son, whom he considered his son, and start a fish farm since, as he put it, "the ocean can't keep feeding us forever." As the state threatened to take his land away, supporters around the country came to his defense, one even composing "The Ballad of Jesse Hardy" to condemn both environmentalists and the state. Hardy eventually relented after a fifteen-hour mediation session and sold in 2005 for 4.95 million dollars.[40]

So what makes the American dream so spellbinding? How does this dream cement a nation of disparate nationalities and ethnicities, and inspire people around the world? More than two decades ago, before the age of the Internet, I asked two students—a woman from the state of New York and a man from Texas—what they had in common, and the woman from New York instantly replied, "Television!" That was a remarkable answer, attesting to the power of the modern media to stitch together a common consciousness, but it was obviously only a half-truth. There is more to what makes Americans American than television networks. One can find clues in American literary and cultural classics; in colonial sermons and the writings of the Founding Fathers; in history books, political treatises, court rulings, and in the tenor of everyday life that eludes inscription. At the risk of sounding too essentialist, I gladly agree with generations of Americans and Europeans alike that there is a *Homo Americanus*, as the acerbic cultural critic H. L. Mencken described America's middle class early in the twentieth century,[41] a human being nurtured in a way of life that is uniquely American. To say this is not to gloss over the historical contradictions and the persecution of the natives, Africans, and indentured servants, or to minimize the arrogance of missionaries and imperialists, but to show that both sides of the fortune divide are uniquely American in ways their fellow humans in other cultures are not.

We have now come to a point where we can have a reasonable sense of American–Muslim relations throughout America's brief but eventful history. America was claimed by a group of chosen people convinced that their new abode was promised to them, just as Zion was promised to the Jews in the Old Testament. Islam, the historic archrival of Christianity, was bound to have a negative effect in this worldview, since it was not only an impediment to the prophecy of restoring Jews to their God-given land to prepare for the return of Christ, but Muslims were also waging maritime *jihads* on American vessels, capturing sailors and demanding ransom. Despite a few positive traits, such as its treatment of slaves and captives, Islam embodied tyranny, fanaticism, and decay. The discovery and exploitation of Arab or Muslim oil didn't change this fundamental perception, since the richest of Arab nations, the oil-rich ones, are only rentiers, not industrial producers or scientific innovators. Neither has America's commitment to Zion changed. Americans managed to give robust support to the Jews when they finally established their nation; John Adams' wish in 1819 was finally fulfilled in 1948. If it was at the expense of non-Jews, that collateral damage had long been anticipated. Restoring Jews to their homeland had always meant removing Muslims and Arabs as unworthy custodians of the Holy Land. Islam has no role in the Bible and is, therefore, an alien presence in America's primordial consciousness.

America has always had commercial interests in the region, but by the middle of twentieth century, it grew dependent on a new Muslim commodity: oil. As the historian Field put it in typical eloquent fashion, "Where once the lamps of the Prophet's temple had been lit by Pennsylvania kerosene, now pipelines and tankers brought this most strategic of commodities from the cradle of civilization to fuel the mechanized societies of the West." And so it came to be that by the 1930s, "the diplomacy of petroleum and the problems presented by a developing Zionism had become principal determinants of American Near Eastern policy."[42]

There is now growing resistance to America's old biblical bias and its dependency on oil. The race for alternative sources of fuel is gaining more speed. Similarly, people inside and outside the United States, Jews and non-Jews alike, are eager to see a permanent resolution of the Israeli–Palestinian question. These voices were particularly strong following Israel's controversial storming of a flotilla carrying aid to the Gaza Strip on international waters in late May 2010. The death of Turkish citizens and the injuries of a number of activists caused an internal uproar, endangered Israel's relations with Turkey, and led supporters to voice their criticism of Israel. Interestingly enough, the late Tony Judt of New York University lumped the oil sheikdoms and Israel together as "America's greatest strategic liability in the Middle East and Central Asia" and called on the United States to "cut through the clichés surrounding it, [and] treat Israel like a 'normal' state and sever the umbilical cord." He might as well have said the "biblical" cord, for that is one of the strongest ties—however strategically cultivated by Israeli leaders in recent decades—that binds the United States to Israel.

The *New York Times* columnist Ross Douthat described Israel, surrounded by Muslim states, as the contemporary equivalent of Outremer, the small principalities left behind by the crusaders in the Middle Ages. Such enclaves lasted longer than Israel has so far existed, but they were eventually overwhelmed by the tides of history and ceased to exist as such. No living entity, human or otherwise, can survive indefinitely in a hostile environment. Only a peaceful arrangement, involving a high degree of sacrifice, could keep Israel from melting into its vast environment and ceasing to exist as a Jewish state. If Israel were to vanish in an ocean of Muslim states, the outcome would, once again, render Jews vulnerable to the gross indignities and injustices they suffered in Christian and Muslim lands for millennia. As bad as it might be for Jews, the nonexistence of Israel would be a catastrophic loss to Muslims and

Arabs because, in my opinion, Muslims cannot find a better model, and even potential ally, than Israel and the Jews. I will say more about this in my final chapter.

Let us, then, recall, before we close this one, that Americans were most successful in the Middle East and Islamic lands when they moderated their dogmas and worked with the local populations to promote their best interests. The Protestant missionaries who sought to bring light and salvation to the region ran against strong hurdles, but they succeeded in introducing modern education and medicine. Americans sacrificed both money and time to support educational institutions in a part of the world that was unfamiliar to them. The historian James Field, whose 1969 account of America in the Mediterranean left no stone unturned, thought that this is a "magnificent record" almost without any "historical parallel."[43] The missionaries laid the ground for the rise of both Turkish and Arab nationalism, either directly through the secular institutions they created, or indirectly, by inspiring Arab immigrant in the United States.

In 1835, Commodore David Porter, an American war hero who had been appointed on a diplomatic mission to Constantinople, predicted that America would have a lasting effect on the Ottoman Empire by introducing modern education. "The march of the intellect which America has everywhere given rise to is sufficient answer to those who assert that she has done no benefit to mankind. The time may come when as great, and as beneficial a change may be produced by her in Turkey, as she has produced on the minds of the greater part of Europe. A reading nation cannot be long in understanding what are its true interests, and when instructed, will not be long in acting on them."[44] More than decade later, Simon Wolf, a Jewish American who had been named consul general to Egypt in 1881, reaffirmed the power of education to liberate Arabs and Muslims, to whom he had expressed gratitude for giving shelter to Jews in earlier centuries: "We must war in the East not with cannon and shot but with schoolbooks, bibles, and constitutions."[45]

Americans had their reasons, of course, but they cared about the fate of Muslim countries. And the feelings were mutual. Muslims and Arabs continued to hold the United States in high esteem well into the twentieth century. When, in 1919, an American commission (the King-Crane Commission) surveyed public opinion throughout much of the old Ottoman provinces, in a line stretching from modern Turkey to Iraq, they reported that the overwhelming majority of people clamored for US mandate over them. (This is exactly what Rev. Rihbany wanted for his native Syria.) The US Congress didn't go for the Commission's recommendation, but the episode is a testament of how much revolutionary Americans had done for all peoples of the Near East and what they could still do for them.[46] "The Americans," Field wrote, "had set out across the world to teach the word of God; quite without intention, as T. E. Lawrence was to observe, they taught revolution."[47] No American organization or policy maker has been able to match this record.

Iran may be implacably opposed to US interventions in its affairs today, but the country has long honored Howard Baskerville, a Presbyterian schoolteacher from Nebraska who taught at the American Memorial School in the ancient city of Tabriz and stood valiantly with the Iranians against British and Russian designs to undermine the Iranians' democratic gains wrested from the corrupt Qajar rulers in 1906. Bakersville was shot dead by a sniper on April 20, 1909, but he remains a revered hero in Iran. Another American, Morgan Shuster, became Treasurer General of Persia in 1911 to help the Iranian government collect taxes, but the Russians and British managed to force him out. Persian poets lauded their hero in verses like "Thou art a part of us, how can we live/apart from thee, O Schuster?"[48]

Just as the United States offers invaluable lessons to Muslims, Americans can do a lot to make sure that their ideals are not lost in the fog of endless war.

Chapter 5

Failing Civilizations

The United States and the Islamic world entered the twenty-first century in a state of murderous conflict, with Muslim terrorists targeting civilians and buildings on American soil, and American troops unleashing their firepower in countries like Afghanistan and Iraq to change regimes and foster democracy. The world was convulsed by such events. Old allies disagreed among themselves about proper strategies to address what seems to be the intractable challenge of dissuading Muslims from engaging in terrorism, promoting democracy and freedom in Muslim-majority nations, and bringing peace to the festering conflict between Israel and the Palestinians.

Supporters lined up on each side of the divide on these burning issues. The United States won the world's heart after 9/11, but soon lost most of its affection. The light of America, the one that Bartholdi wanted to immortalize with his Statue of Liberty, shone brightly for a short time but was soon covered by the darkening clouds of global discontent. And the crisis of Muslim-majority nations, long buried under the passion of loyalty to tradition and howling protests against the depredations of imperialists of all sorts, was suddenly displayed for the whole world to behold.

The US intervention in Iraq was not without its advantages to the Iraqis, particularly to the long-suffering Kurds and Shiites, but the region, as whole, remains in a state of dangerous limbo. No prophet can foresee a better future under such circumstances. There is simply no option to a radical change in minds and attitudes, among Americans and Muslims alike, if we hope to save our collective human heritage from more unnecessary tragedies. Both Muslims and Americans need to reassess their beliefs and attitudes, as Obama rightly enjoined us to do in 2009, if we hope to make any progress at all. By the time President Obama made his remarks, it was clear that Muslims had failed to deal with their history objectively and work toward a better future. The United States, meanwhile, had forfeited its role of inspiring leader as it embraced economic policies that were on the verge of ruining the revolutionary legacy that gave birth to the American nation. With the onset of the age of colonialism and oil in the twentieth century, as well as the establishment of Israel, America's image in the Muslim world had been radically transformed. Only by taking stock of our common histories and realize the extent to which we have lost control of our destinies, we may perhaps begin to build a better future together.

American presidents, including George W. Bush, who had the misfortune of dealing with the worst ravages of extremism and terror, have always said the right things about Islam. They usually exonerate the religion from the acts of extremists and insist that Islam is a religion of peace. But it was only with the election of Barack Hussein Obama that the tone began to change noticeably. He acknowledged America's mistakes in the past, called on Muslims to promote freedom and democracy, and asked Israel to give up its occupied Palestinian lands for a durable piece. He seemed to suggest that Americans fought not for independence from the world, but from political tyranny. The founders of the United States, much like Obama himself, were cosmopolitan people who appealed to the "Opinion of Mankind" and wanted to be part of the community of nations, not disengage from world affairs. This may be why Obama insisted that the United States was not fighting Islam and, in Cairo, reminded the world that it was the Muslim nation of Morocco that first welcomed the fledgling republic into the community of nations.

When Obama first addressed Muslims, whether from the White House, Turkey, or Egypt, he was riding a wave of high popularity across the globe, including in the Muslim world. Moroccans had set up support groups during his presidential campaign, and when he became president, the Muslims' enthusiasm knew almost no bounds. Celebrations erupted everywhere, including in war-torn Iraq. By the time he addressed them in their home countries, he appeared as their last best hope for a comprehensive solution to the long clashes that pitted both communities against each other for so long.

This spontaneous and genuine burst of enthusiasm didn't last long, as history resumed its tortuous course. A little more than a year after his memorable Cairo speech, a global survey conducted by the Pew Research Center showed Egyptians had the worst favorable view of the United States in the previous five years, declining considerably from the time Obama was elected and spoke to them. Obama continued to enjoy high ratings in Europe and other parts of the world, but not among his own citizens at home or with Muslims abroad. With trouble continuing in Iraq and Afghanistan, and the situation in a stalemate in Israel and Palestine, Muslims realized, once again, that American presidents were dedicated first and foremost to their national interests, however well or badly understood these interests might be.

What was even more startling to me in the results of the Pew poll was the possibility that the United States in the last few years of George W. Bush may have had been more favorably viewed by Egyptians. Later that summer, another poll of four thousand people in Egypt, Saudi Arabia, Morocco, Lebanon, Jordan, and the United Arab Emirates (UAE), conducted by the University of Maryland and Zobgy International, further confirmed the Arabs' dimming view of Obama, their despair over an equitable resolution of the Israeli—Palestinian conflict, their growing support for Iran's right to have its own nuclear program, and the popularity of the Turkish prime minister Recep Tayyip Erdogan, who had stood up to Israel earlier in the year. Islam was shown to be growing in strength, as Moroccans and Saudis were more likely to identify as Muslims than citizens of their own nations. Arab opinion of the United States and Obama kept getting worse, even if the United States was so clearly on the side of antigovernment protesters. Another poll by Zogby International conducted in May and June of 2011 reaffirmed the previous year's findings. If we ever needed proof that things do not change overnight, both polls showed it with unmistakable clarity in 2010 and 2011. By the time President Obama addressed Indonesians and Muslims from Jakarta in November 2010, Muslims had already dismissed him as all talk and no action.[1] Even his Mideast speech of May 19, 2011, with its eloquent support of democratic uprisings throughout the Arab world and advocacy for a two-state solution along the 1967 lines in Palestine, failed to impress Muslim audiences.

Does this mean, however, that President Obama wasn't genuine about bringing peace to the Middle East? I doubt that. I am

convinced that he is a genuine peace seeker who was caught in the
much stronger forces of history, memory, and politics. He could not,
single-handedly, reverse centuries of prejudice, antagonism, skirmishes, and even wars between his nation and the Muslim world.
The view of Islam as the antithesis of the American way of life that
spread after 9/11 had, as we saw, a much older pedigree in the culture. It was a common belief among America's founding Protestants.
To them, Islam was an abomination to be eradicated. Islam's Prophet
Mohammed was an impostor who waged wars and indulged in sen-
sual pleasures. Muslim rulers were barbaric despots who ruled over a
craven and ruthless people. Muslims were no more than bandits and
pirates who took good Americans captive.

This early and highly prejudiced Protestant impulse meshed seamlessly with the secular revolutionary ethos of 1776 and gave birth to
America's evangelical mission to convert and change the world in
its own image. Muslims, like Roman Catholics and other Christians
in the Middle East, were a fallen lot who needed to be saved through
the Protestant faith. The same was true of nations, whether European or Muslim, who were languishing in slavery and oppression.
They needed America's political and economic model to uplift their
societies and join the community of civilized nations. With very few
exceptions—and only when such exceptions could be used as foils
to score political points at home—did Islam appear benevolent and a
worthy religion. In all this history of anti-Islamic sentiments, Americans never really had a visceral hatred of Islam, or of anyone else,
for that matter. They just believed that their religious and political
systems were the best that had ever been created. Given the huge
transformations they initiated, they could be excused for thinking
of themselves as God's real Chosen People. Humility doesn't come
easy to the strong and successful.

How, then, do we think of a better future, without rehashing the
worn pieties that lead nowhere? When humans fall ill, remedial and
preventive measures need to restore body and mind to health. Nothing lasts forever, of course, as people from the ancient civilizations
of the Middle East well know; but, by the same token, cultural habits have a way of lingering over centuries and millennia. A people
are shaped by their historical circumstances more than they are by
their genes. From a strictly biological point of view, Puritans are not
different from Anglicans, nor are Jews separate from Muslims. A
Puritan, Protestant, Jew, or Muslim is someone who is molded by

certain cultural and political traditions; he or she is not a different brand of human species. If skin color is not a biological divider, neither is religion.

The question, then, that hovers over us now is whether we have the ability to recalibrate the traditions that shape us. For it is quite clear that supremacist attitudes—whether religious, cultural, or, for those who still cling to the antiquated notion, racial—are not conducive to peace and stability. Humanity has built edifices to knowledge, science, and the arts, but humans are still trapped in the same passions that were the daily lot of nations with limited literacy and knowledge of outsiders. We may very well be trapped in our biological passions, but I still believe that variations in human conduct and aspirations give us a spectrum of choices. Emotions, like appetites, may be real, but the way we manage (or feed) them is shaped by cultural and social traditions and expectations. I have lived in the United States more than half my life, yet a day rarely goes by when I don't experience bits of culture shock, even though I consider myself comfortably integrated in this society. Because my basic worldview was shaped in the Moroccan city of Tangier, I continue to learn and adjust to what comes naturally to my American-born children. I often wonder whether, socially speaking, my children and I share the same values. The point I am trying to make is that cultural influences are as significant as biological ones. Both can be modified to some extent, although I know from experience that they can't be radically altered.

We may not be able to grasp the better angels of our nature, but not trying to do so undermines the very notion of education itself. Which self-respecting human being alive today does not value a good education? People spend huge amounts of money on educating their young, but how many of us think about what a good education means? Making a living in an increasingly uncertain economy is certainly a powerful motive, but shouldn't creating a more humane global civilization be an equally strong incentive? Leaving your children huge amounts of wealth in a broken economic and social system is like providing them with luxurious condominiums in a maximum-security prison. If the best-educated people in the world—the best engineers, philosophers, health care professionals, lawyers, and writers—live in hostile environments plagued by bad bridges, poverty, illness, injustice, and a declining taste for literature, the best they could do is hide behind barricades of privilege and watch the world around them drift into further turmoil. There is no doubt, in my mind, that caring for one's children means caring about what kind of future we leave them. And to do so, we must be willing to look critically at what works and what doesn't, not just for the narrow interests of a nation or faith, but for the whole well-being of our shrinking planet. In the case of relations between United States and Muslim-majority nations, we have no better guide than history to diagnose strengths and weaknesses. The Muslim and American bodies need to be strengthened for the two to have a better appreciation of each other.

Let us begin with the case of Islam. There is barely a person on our planet who hasn't been aware of this religion, and many non-Muslims have some idea that Islam is a singularly regressive faith, with adherents sporting long, shaggy beards and women draped in head-to-toe robes, not to mention those whose faces that are hidden from view. The face of Islam, to the chagrin of many modern Muslims, is medieval. It suggests that Muslims have decided that all norms have been established once and for all in the distant past, whether such norms involve the content of faith or social customs. They believe that the Qur'an is the literal word of God communicated to the Prophet Mohammed through the archangel Gibreel and that their civilization enjoyed a Golden Age of power and prosperity that lasted, more or less, till the collapse of the Ottoman Empire and the abolition of the Caliphate in 1924. The bad condition of Muslims today is attributed to the abandonment of pure Islam—perhaps one, like the Wahhabi cult, that is stripped of accretions and corrupting influences—and selling out to the West. We are led to conclude that had Islam not been diluted and the West not colonized Muslim lands, Muslims today would be much better off. Cleansing Islam and Muslim lands is, therefore, a necessary condition to restore a new Muslim Golden Age of power and prosperity.

To hope for a better future is a reasonable aspiration, but the diagnosis of Muslim ills is more feel-good self-deception than a sober-eyed look at the Muslim condition. What lessons could be learned from the vast history of Muslim peoples to plan for the kind of development that makes nations stronger? Most nations and civilizations were mighty at one time or another—the Greeks, the Romans, ancient Egypt, Persia, Iraq, the list is long—and all lost their powerful status. Would it make sense for these nations to go back to their ancient histories to build stronger nations for the twenty-first century? The best they could do is learn from the mistakes that led to their stagnation and downfall.

Spending centuries lamenting decline and oppression will not move Muslims ahead. Not only that, Muslims are better advised to think of themselves as members of one human community, not as another chosen people with an exclusive religion. This may sound harsh, but if Muslims could claim a more global identity with the same fervor they embrace their seventh-century religion, they would have the potential of being world leaders and pioneers of change. But to think about the collective wellbeing of humanity requires that we look critically at the beliefs that have prevented us from expanding beyond our narrow frames of self-reference.

A good starting point would be to decide whether religions are supernatural events or the expression of humans in history. This is not to say that what humans invent is not sacred; in my view, that's the very meaning of sacredness, although we attribute such creations to deities and higher powers. Questioning a people's religion doesn't mean belittling their faith, for we all live by faith in one thing or another. Those who say that one religion or culture is better than another are expressing a fundamentalist view; they are not making logical or nuanced historical assessments. Qualifiers like "advanced" do not mean much, either, since, like Gross Domestic Product statistics, they measure one aspect of progress (such as better technology and a longer life span), but they don't seem to focus on the negative (such as violence and environmental degradation). A high-tech society could be emotionally impoverished and socially primitive, while a society of strong human bonds and great cuisine could be lagging in educational attainment and personal freedoms. No one model fits all, but a critical approach that maximizes human fulfillment in any context is what is needed across the board.

If we agree that purity is fiction—and a dangerous one at that—we may then proceed to look at ways Muslims could change their attitudes toward the past in order to build a better future. The first thing to do is realize that Islam is a mélange of cultures, not a pure invention. New ideas usually appear in cosmopolitan settings, places where different cultures and religions meet, as in Mecca of the seventh century. Arabic, the privileged language of the Qur'an, is much like English or French today: it contains a good number of words of non-Arabic origin. The Muslims' holy book is part of much older

Oriental traditions and shares common themes with them, which may explain why the Muslim tradition was so eager to discredit non-Muslim cultures and religions as either heathenish or, if biblical, corrupt. The Umayyad and Abbasid dynasties waged what the French-Tunisian scholar Mondher Sfar called a "scorched-earth policy" on history, erasing, with few exceptions, anything prior to Mohammed's apostolate at the age of forty. They mystified the production of the Qur'an and used the *sunna* to destroy and reconstruct the holy book. Consequently, few know that Mohammed was tempted to sin once or twice, or that his companions must have consumed wine. Islamic traditions froze an ancient world, including God himself, and made it our own. Instead of seeing God and the Qur'an itself as reflections of their times, early Islamic regimes sacralized them and turned any inquiry that contradicted these beliefs into criminal offenses. This erasure of pre-Islamic history also explains why most Muslims know virtually nothing about the religions and civilizations that preceded the birth of Islam. If they did, they'd realize that the opening chapter of the Qur'an, a sort of preface, the *fatiha,* is almost a verbatim reproduction of the first psalm of the Bible and the Seven Sleepers tale echoes one in the Hindu epic of the *Mahabharta*.[2]

Raising the issue of the Qur'an is important because we all know that it is the "mother of all books" when it comes to sacred Islamic artifacts and traditions. The Qur'an is certainly a very inspiring liturgical document, one that is meant to be recited or read (hence its Syriac name, the *qur'an*), but its contents should certainly be open to all kinds of readings and interpretations. The Qur'an is, therefore, the litmus test of what is and is not permissible in the Muslim intellectual tradition. The freedom to read and interpret the Qur'an in Muslim-majority nations as one sees fit would mean that citizens of those nations are no longer governed by the sacred and that they are willing to live and let live. For to live in societies with multiple faiths and opinions makes all belief systems stronger and more meaningful. It means that one has thought about them and has chosen them out of conviction. It doesn't mean that one is bound to a belief or position forever, but that no one is coerced either by state authorities or through social pressure to live in a state of spiritual or intellectual hypocrisy.

Islam borrowed liberally from both Jewish and Christian traditions to create its own rituals and holidays. After the death of Prophet Mohammed in 632, Muslims fanned out in crusades against neighboring civilizations, capturing Damascus, Jerusalem, the Sassanid capital, Ctesiphon, Alexandria in Egypt, and so on. As the Muslim empire and the Arab Umayyad dynasty moved its center from Arabia to Damascus, an old Byzantine city, foreign ideas and influences started shaping Islamic law and ethics. Islamic architecture—whether that of mosques or baths (*hammams*)—was inspired by Greek, Roman, and Byzantine models. Muslim cities incorporated several Roman designs while agriculture borrowed from Babylonians, Greeks, Romans, Syrians, Byzantines, and Iberians. Muslims universalized Indian numbers and transmitted parts of Greek learning. Even religious traditions, such as Sufism (mysticism), are inspired by pre-Islamic practices.

This is the way of all civilizations—they grow and flourish through mixing, sharing, and borrowing. This is what allowed Islamic civilization to develop and reach its apogee. The extreme anxiety about the West doesn't make much sense if we remember that Islam was built on the back of older civilizations. The denunciation of soccer, music, and even hairstyles by leaders in Muslim communities around the world today are symptoms of severely deranged minds. For which human being living today could function without relying on the product of Western science? Which Muslim extremist can operate without using a cell phone or the Internet?

Not surprisingly, it was during the period of Islam's relaxed adaptation—say, between 750 and 1050—that Muslims enjoyed an amazing freedom of thought in their approach to religion. Writers like Ibn al-Muqaffaʿ (720–756), who adapted *Kalila wa Dimna* from older Persian fables, valued reason and dissociated morals from religion. For him, an atheist (*mulhid*) can be as virtuous as anyone else. Few people, he believed, are able to justify their beliefs because most believers either inherit their faith from their parents, are coerced into it, or they have some benefit in being part of the faith. Ibn al-Muqaffaʿ criticized the Qur'an, the imposture of prophets, and all of monotheism. Others like Hunayn Ibn Is'haq (808–873), the "freethinker" Al-Warraq (died c. 861), Abu Bakr Razi (c. 854– c. 925) all privileged reason over revelation. Razi, one of the world's most influential physicians, thought that prophets were mentally unbalanced and that rituals produce maniacs obsessed by imagined impurities. The liberal school of theologians known as Muʿtazila tried to keep the art of argumentation alive in the ninth century, but they were excluded from royal patronage as more conservative

forces displaced them. By the fourteenth century, scholars like Ibn
Taymiyya (1263–1328) were denouncing all innovative thought as
bid'a. With few exceptions, this has been the situation in the Muslim
world ever since. Muslim reformers have been helpless against this
onslaught on reason; they spend as much time defending their Islamic
credentials as they do proposing cautious proposals for change.[3]

The renowned Muslim legal scholar Abdullahi Ahmed An-Na'im
has made a convincing case that for a Muslim to be truly Muslim,
out of choice and without coercion, he or she needs to live in a
secular state. It is the only way for the Golden Rule of reciprocity
(*mu'awada*) to have meaning. The Shari'a, the product of human
interpretation of the Qur'an and the Sunna (prophetic traditions),
may shape attitudes and policies, but they cannot be the basis of
government, and must be kept in check by what An-Na'im calls
"civic reason," one that includes all citizens of the nation-state.
Reinterpreting the Shari'a is also indispensable. If one recalls that
the Shari'a is "the result of intergenerational consensus since the
seventh century," one could make the case of replacing one form of
consensus with another. Speaking as a Muslim, An-Na'im believes
that it is "necessary" to "reinterpret Islamic sources in order to affirm
and protect the freedom of religion and belief." For if certain provi-
sions in the Shari'a—such as the supremacy of men over women,
the status of the *dhimma*, and aggressive *jihad*—are not corrected,
"their moral and emotional impact on Muslims will severely undermine the ethos of constitutionalism, human rights, and citizenship."
This is why, I guess, An-Na'im wants Muslims to "safeguard the
psychological and social as well as political possibility of heresy and
disagreement among its members" because only then can Muslims
be true Muslims.[4]

Looked at from a secular perspective, early Islamic history, with
its prophet, leaders, and protagonists, is no better or worse than any
other people's history. It had its share of glory as well as bloodcurdling monstrosities. But if we accept the thesis—as I do—that
humans make their own history, then we must account for the
backwardness of Muslim-majority nations without hiding behind
air-brushed accounts of a Golden Age. With the excommunication
of Averroes in the twelfth century, philosophical thought, already
under siege following the demotion of the Mu'tazilites, ended in
Islam and took off in Christian Europe. Before too long, Islam was
banished from Europe and Europeans were crisscrossing the seas

in search of trade and new lands. The Muslim mind, meanwhile, remained trapped in the tyranny of the divine, unable to shake off the package of laws that had been inflicted on it in the first centuries of Islam. While Europeans kept pushing the limits of what is intellectually possible, Muslims sought what is theologically permissible and retreated into a debilitating orthodoxy that made them increasingly weaker. This is how Americans first encountered Islam and continue to do so today. Muslim-majority nations have ever looked despotic and beholden to archaic notions of the sacred.

When Islamists, as well as many ordinary Muslims, invoke the Golden Age of Islam, that is the era of the Prophet Mohammed, his four political successors, collectively known as the Righteous Caliphs, and the first two dynasties of Islam (the Umayyads and Abbasids) as models for the future, they probably have a highly romanticized view of that history, one that has been hallowed by the repeated sermons and incantations of religious scholars. Knowing that history, as history, not as myth, may, in fact, help Muslims see beyond their American or Western boogeyman and understand that only they—and they alone—can make themselves break free from servitude, especially the mental kind, which is the worst. For even if the United States and the West were concocting nefarious designs on the Muslim world, a freer Muslim mind, not one terrorized by sacred myths, is likely to be more effective in fighting such schemes. Contemporary Muslims must know that they never had an ideal political system, one that is just and fair to all, if they want to imagine one that really works for all people. In fact, the issue of good governance, one that enables people to be productive as well as creative, a system that protects people as well as their ideas and property, has been elusive for so long that people finally erupted in the demonstrations that led to Arab Spring of 2011. I am afraid, however, that real change may take much longer than a spring or two.

During the Prophet's lifetime, violence against critics and enemies characterized the consolidation of the early Muslim community, with the prophet himself leading the way. After Mohammed's flight (*hijra*) from Mecca to Medina in 622 (which marks year one in the Islamic calendar), the Jewish tribes of Medina (Qaynuqa, Nadir, and Qurayzah), who refused to accept Mohammed's prophecy, or to support his mission, were subjected to a ruthless policy of ethnic cleansing.[5] The Jews were either expelled without their possessions, or after felling their palm trees (a war crime by Arab custom), or they were simply slaughtered en masse, their women and children collected and sold as booty. Mohammed also fought Meccans tenaciously and broke a ceasefire brokered at Al-Hudaybiyah in 628 to conquer Mecca and eventually subdue all of Arabia. The Ka'ba and the Hajj were afterward Islamized; the Jews and Christians were excluded. Such policies helped Mohammed unite Arabia, engage in expansionist missions, impose poll taxes (*jizya*) on non-Muslims (beginning with the Jews of Nadir), and establish a central absolutist authority before he died in 632. During this eventful life, the Prophet had thirteen wives (including the daughters of his two faithful companions, Abu Bakr and Omar, as well as the wife of his adopted son Zayd ibn Harithah) and many slave girls.

The Prophet died without leaving a will (he may have been deliberately prevented from doing so), and so his disciples fell on each other with lightning speed. After Abu Bakr's brief reign, Omar took over and was stabbed to death. His successor, Othman, successively husband to two of Mohammed's daughters, the Umayyad known for assembling the Qur'an into one authoritative volume, was so corrupt and nepotistic that Abu Bakr's son (adopted by Ali) and his men stormed his gaudy palace in Medina, killed him, and severed his Syrian wife's arms and fingers. The next caliph, Ali, spent his reign fighting the prophet's wife Aisha; the Umayyad governor of Syria, Mu'awiya; and his own disillusioned supporters, one of whom smote him to death with a poisoned sword in 661. Ali's two sons were deliberately kept out of power. The eldest, Hassan, was bribed away by Mu`awiya, and the second, Hussein, was massacred and beheaded, along with his supporters, in what is now Karbala in Iraq. Many of Hussein's male descendants were also killed.[6]

Just as the Umayyads created the early foundations of an Islamic civilization that would reach Spain, they also consolidated the institutional tyranny and bloodshed that have characterized politics in Islamic lands ever since. As noted above, the assassination of leaders began in earnest soon after Mohammed's death and continued apace during the last decade of the Umayyad reign. The head of caliph Al-Walid II (743–744) was offered to his challenger Yazid III (744) following a *coup d'état*. Yazid III died the same year, replaced by Marwan II (744–750), who then had the corpse of his predecessor exhumed and nailed on a cross. Marwan II was to be the last of the Umayyads before the Abbasids, tracing their lineage of the Prophet's uncle Al-'Abbas and invoking the authority of Ali's nephew Abu

Hisham to overthrow the Umayyad tyrants. Thus Marwan II was killed in Egypt in 750 and his head sent to Abu al-'Abbas as-Saffah, the first Abbasid leader. As-Saffah orchestrated a reconciliation party with leading Umayyads only to massacre all guests, except one, 'Abd ar-Rahman, who fled to North Africa (home of his Berber wife), then to Spain, where he established the Umayyad caliphate of Cordoba.

The dynasty that stopped this sordid state of affairs, the Abbasids, moved their center to Iraq and built a great civilization, with its center in their jewel city of Baghdad. Greek philosophy was translated even as heretics and contrarians were persecuted for their unorthodox views. Influenced by Persian culture, letters flourished. Islamic law was developed while philosophers and thinkers argued about how best to read the Qur'an without falling out of the faith. Within short order, however, the Abbasid Empire grew into a failed state. Caliphs were isolated, while their viziers governed and palace intrigues multiplied. The caliphs drafted foreign mercenaries (Turks and Slavs) into the army and raised taxes to support military spending. Corruption and the neglect of basic infrastructure further impoverished Iraq, which would not recover until the twentieth century. Islamic power would never be quite the same after the fall of the Abbasids. Soon philosophical inquiry would be discredited and political absolutism, in alliance with docile religious scholars, would imprison the Muslim mind in a stultifying culture of fear despotism. There are lessons here for both Muslims and Americans today.

Interestingly, in looking for solutions to their political weakness in the last two centuries, Muslim Arabs alternated between the Umayyad model and the Abbasid one. Because the Umayyads were ethnically Arab and tried to maintain their Arab distinctiveness, they appealed to the aspirations of Arab nationalists. The Abbasid Empire, which included non-Arabs, remains, on the other hand, the model for Pan-Islamists. But neither the Umayyad nor the Abbasid political regime provide models for the kind of equality and justice that Muslims crave today. The post-Prophetic era in Islam was certainly no golden political age, and it certainly was not divine in any sense of the word. Living in a state of fear is not an act of grace, and yet, as the *Economist* reported in late 2010 (just before the outbreak of mass demonstrations across the Arab world), Muslims, and Arabs in particular, continue to live in some of the most despotic countries in the world.[7] While Arab Christians in Iraq are threatened with extinction by the fury of Islamic extremists in that country, no Muslim action is taken to stop the horror. No international meetings are being held in Mecca to stop this cultural genocide. Consoled by self-serving notions of the divine, the vast majority Muslims simply can't see or feel the violence they are inflicting on others.

The exaggeration of the divine, or the sacred, in Muslim life is what early Muslim heretics (the *zanadiqa*) complained about and tried to disabuse people of. Their legacy is now almost forgotten, but there can be no progress in the Islamic world if the practice of religion continues to infringe on the unfettered activity of the mind. Muslims are used to a long menu of prohibitions and *fatwas*, with some seeking legal opinions on the most absurd of matters. This shows that religion in the Islamic world discourages thinking for oneself, or, as the old Muslim heretics and their eighteenth-century European counterparts, the radical philosophers of the Enlightenment, would say, from using reason. The Muslim's reliance on religious scholars on how to eat and which hand to use first perpetuates a state of fear and infantilism in the Muslim mind. Urban Muslims living in big cities may excel in fields like engineering, but their approach to religion remains no different from the illiterate farmer's, or even their medieval fellow coreligionist. Scientific know-how, or applied science, goes hand in hand with archaic cultural habits. It's as if the realm of religious inquiry, through philosophy or revisionist history, were simply quarantined and made off-limits.

Even though this mindset is what has kept Muslims behind most of the world today, that is the one subject that is almost never addressed by scholars and intellectuals who are committed to a better future for the Muslim world. Or if they do, they are not quite sure what to do about it. In his 1916 book, *The Disintegration of Islam*, based on lectures delivered the previous year at Princeton and other venues, the influential American missionary Samuel Zwemer recorded the frustration and helplessness of Muslims trying to reverse their decline. In 1899, for instance, Muslims assembled in Mecca to diagnose the ills of their civilization, but they couldn't contemplate breaking away from what Zwemer diagnosed as "the dead weight of tradition."[8] Obviously, we need to take Zwemer's interest with a grain of salt, since his goal was to discredit Islam and promote his brand of Christianity, but the missionary got the part of tradition right. Islam's insistence of the observance of rituals and tradition works against a culture of criticism and freedom. And although many, at the time, tended to read the Saudi-based Wahhabi movement as closer to the Protestant spirit, Zwemer would not have none of that: "Luther," he wrote, "emancipated the intellect; Abd-ul-Wahab enchained it."[9] By 1902, some thinkers, like the Indian Mohammed Sarfaran Khan, could tell that Islam had no option but to join the train of Western civilization. Khan wanted to modify the number and timing of prayers, relax ablution and Ramadan rules, and end polygamy, among other measures.[10]

Such half-measures remained quixotic, however, and had no impact. In 1930, the Syrian Lebanese writer, Shakib Arslan (1869–1946) asked the same question in his aptly titled book, *Why Have Muslims Fallen Behind, and Why Have Others Forged Ahead*? It is a question that has haunted the Muslim mind for two centuries, but the answer continues to elude us today, partly because few Muslims are willing to trespass on the culture's lines in the sand, the red lines drawn in ever concentric circles around the Muslim mind.

Perhaps, as the Israeli scholar Dan Diner believes, the Muslim body needs an "intervention," because, like addicts of all sorts, Muslims need an external jumpstart in order to move again. I am sure many Muslims reading the preceding sentence are probably thinking that the scholar who wants to take on the ghosts haunting the Muslim mind is in no position to advise Muslims, since Israel, the occupier of Arab lands, has its own share of people who are governed by the sacred. In fact, it's well accepted now that nonreligious ideologies, such as Zionism or nationalism *tout court*, have their own sacred motifs, which is why people go to war and kill each other.

Be that as it may, what interests me in Diner's diagnosis, supported by select readings in history, is that he shows how the power of the sacred prevented Muslims from being active players in modern civilization. Like the UN-sponsored Arab Human Development reports issued during the first decade of the twenty-first century, which depict the abysmal social conditions in Muslim-majority Arab lands, Diner's book is motivated by the desire to see Arab and Muslim societies do better, move ahead, become healthier, and get more international respect. If, for Diner, the first Arab Human Development Report (AHDR)—which *Time* magazine named Book of the Year in 2002—is a "revolutionary manifesto,"[11] a call for reform whose model is inescapably the West, then the second AHDR of 2003 goes even further and calls for the uprooting of superstition from the Muslim Arab mind through the promotion of scientific values.[12]

Arabs have variously blamed their predicament on the Europeans, Ottomans, and the State of Israel for the trauma of occupation and humiliation, but few are willing to probe deeper into the causes of what Arslan called Muslim backwardness. Ever since Muslims came into shocking contact with the more developed Europeans, the best they could do was import European technologies and know-how to strengthen the powers of the state, while judiciously trying to keep secularization, with its culture of research, as well as the rule of law, at bay. People, therefore, have grown distrustful of government and Muslim-majority Arab states remain poor despite their massive natural resources. The discovery of oil only intensified the culture of corruption and despotism since the wealth it generated further widened the gap between the people and their rulers.

Because of the power of the scared, Diner argues, Muslims lost multiple opportunities to change with their times and so became passive players in modern history, their fate decided for them by others. For instance, the Ottomans paid scant attention to the discovery of the New World, but they were still dramatically and, more importantly, fatefully affected by the impact of this event. The flow of America's precious metals—silver and gold—into Europe upset the traditional balance of trade and helped give rise to a mercantilist social order in Western Europe. The discovery was part of a process allowing European Christian merchants (God and gold went together for centuries) to circumnavigate the land routes controlled by Muslims. In 1497—only five years after Columbus's first voyage— Vasco de Gama circumnavigated the Cape of Good Hope. Four years later (1501), the Dutch city of Antwerp received its first shipment of Asian spices from the Portuguese. Sea transportation was faster and cheaper (fewer tax barriers, although the Ottomans tried to control ports on the Arabian peninsula to tax ships in transit). By 1571, the Ottomans couldn't withstand Europe's might and suffered the devastating defeat at the Battle of Lepanto. In short, the highly centralized, conservative Ottoman state was poorly equipped to cope with the earthshaking events that flowed from the rise of a new social and economic order in Western Europe and was, therefore, set in a long process of decline, despite future military conquests.

Printing provides another example of the Muslims' false choices. Ever since Johannes Gutenberg invented the printing press with its movable type, thereby accelerating the acquisition of knowledge and enabling the Reformation as well as the Renaissance, Muslims leaders kept printing at bay, issuing bans against it, or, if allowed, confining it to the domain of the profane, which was limited indeed. The printing press, with its mechanical prowess of reproduction, spearheaded an industry that facilitated a new (perhaps independent) approach to knowledge and the divine. In this way, Diner says, "all the hallmarks of an incipient modernity were implicit in the printed book."[13]

Jews and Christians in the Ottoman Empire embraced such technology at once, but not Muslims. The Ottoman sultan Bayesid II banned printing in 1485. Books printed in Arabic (in Italy) were allowed to be sold in 1588, but there were no buyers. In 1727, Sultan Ahmed III allowed the printing of books, but excluded any books with religious themes, which meant most of them. In 1747, the printing house was shut down. In 1784 a censorship council was set up under Sultan Abdulhamid I. Thus, the first printings of the Qur'an were undertaken by Christians in non-Muslim lands. (The first version to be printed by Muslims for Muslims was in 1828 in Teheran.) By the early nineteenth century, American and British missionaries in Malta rationalized and standardized the printing of Arabic, printed the first Arabic grammar, and therefore helped spark the Arab Renaissance, or *nahda*. The use of "hot-metal composition with movable type" in printing the Qur'an continued, however, to be banned and the holy book was printed lithographically to preserve "the impression of the handwritten original, leaving the aura of the sacred attaching to it undisturbed."[14] This is still the case today.

The emergence of history as "change through time" in the early modern period (if such Eurocentric categories hold), and the withdrawal of God, so to speak, from the narrative, "reshaped in worldly terms the older salvational notion of a self-fulfilling future."[15] This future, or telos, could only be achieved through means of "development." If one accepts the notion that the secularization of history is intimately tied to the process of development, we would understand why the primacy of the sacred law in Islam, and its insistence on retrieving an ideal "time of origin," a "*past* utopia,"[16] a perfect polity that existed in ancient times and that perpetually serves as the model to strive for, is hampering the Muslims' intellectual takeoff.

What explains this strong penchant for arresting or freezing time—if not reversing it altogether? The realities of the material world? Or the reverse? Diner thinks it's "preferable to speak of an affinity between material conditions and their sacred underpinnings."

In any case, in Muslim societies, space and time are absorbed by the sacred, expressed in the form of immutable law. Even cities, like Jerusalem, are simply named "the holy" in Arabic, *Al-Quds*.[17]

Jews, whose religion is also one of law, struggled with the same issues, but their diasporic and exilic condition prepared them to live within two laws, or spheres: the profane laws of whatever land they happen to be in, and the dictates of Jewish, or sacred, law. This modus vivendi evolved into secularization, if you will; but Islam didn't benefit from a similar experience and has remained a "political religion." (To be sure, many prominent Jewish scholars didn't feel comfortable with the "Potestantizing" of their faith or with the contradictions of the Enlightenment and preferred the Islamic insistence on the divine or medieval rationalism.)[18]

The Jews' struggles with modernity are too complex and time and culture specific to be of much relevance to Islam today; but what is important to remember is that it was the Diaspora with its dual or multiple allegiances that opened the way to the renaissance of Judaism in the twentieth century. It is, therefore, not surprising that Diner sees hope in Muslim minorities in the West, particularly those in the United States, where, for the sake of public interest or common good (*maslaha*), a new Muslim law of minorities (*fiqh al-aqalliyyat*), first issued as a *fatwa* in 1994 by Tahar Jabir al-Alwani, which replaces *dar al-harb* with *dar al-da'wa*.[19]

Could American Muslim minorities, or even European ones, as Gilles Kepel sees it, be the vanguard for a new Islamic renaissance, one that would strengthen Muslim-majority nations and make them meaningful contributors to our global civilization? In his farewell speech in 2003, Malaysia's outspoken prime minister, Mahathir bin Mohamad, addressing Muslims, including heads of state, said, "Whether we like it or not, we have to change, not by changing our religion but by applying its teachings in the context of a world that is radically different from that of the first Islamic century." Not only that, the man who had blamed the Jews for causing the financial crisis a few years earlier asked Muslims to imitate the Jews: "They survived 2000 years of pogroms not by hitting back, but by thinking."[20]

To be truly emancipated, people in Muslim-majority nations must feel free to think and express themselves about any subject they want, including the most scared of subjects, the Qur'an itself. In the last few centuries, Protestants, Jews, and later Catholics all had to come to terms with what is called biblical criticism. But the Muslims, once again, remain alone among these religious traditions in not producing a similar scholarly approach. Since the Mu´tazila were defeated and the dogma of an uncreated and eternal Qur'an became established, Qur'anic criticism has simply not existed. A few scholars have made valiant efforts, but they have remained marginal. This intellectual taboo has hampered philological criticism of the Qur'anic text. Because it is considered the word of God, not a historical expression, collected and published in book form by humans over a long period of time spanning centuries, Muslim scholars remain stymied by their cultural taboos.

Yet any educated Muslim who has analyzed a text or a speech knows all too well that books don't materialize miraculously from the sky, that they must be composed first, assembled, edited, and published in a process that involves many humans working together, or separately, over time. All scripture—Jewish, Christian, and Muslim—was produced in a very elaborate human process, whose ultimate goal was to attribute authorship not to the actual producers but to an abstract God. Scripture, in this sense, is merely another human-made idol referring to an all-seeing but unseen deity. Saying this publicly in a Muslim society is, however, tantamount to a criminal offense, one that could cause a person his or her life, because we are led to believe that the Muslim mind, like a child's relationship with Santa Claus, is not ready to face up to the possibility that the concept of the Qur'anic God, inherited from Judaism and Christianity, is a human invention. The anxiety is understandable because, as the scholar F. E. Peters stated, "To rule man into Scripture is, in that precise degree, to rule God out."[21] Dodging this question indefinitely, however, will only keep the minds of thinkers in Muslim-majority nations in chains. A little thinking would convince devout Muslims that critical studies of the Qur'anic text would not take away from the faith of those who have chosen their religion out of conviction. Tens of millions of Americans are devout Christians despite the endless books disproving the truth of Christianity or even the existence of God published in the United States. Christian literalists are even unmoved by Charles Darwin's theory of evolution, even though it is a cornerstone of any serious course in biology.

Muslims or Western scholars of Islam would read such challenges to Islam as unfair, since the West, or the United States, in particular, has little understanding of the Muslim faith or the aspirations of its people. These positions reflect the two sides' commitments to their faith or subject, but they don't help us chart a way out of the debilitating weakness of Muslim-majority societies. The American or European scholars who study Islam from well-endowed Western institutions may care genuinely about Islam and its people, but few would trade their universities, libraries, or freedoms for those in Muslim societies. That is totally understandable. The brain drain and capital flight from Muslim-majority nations to the West are high. If people are not free and secure in their possessions, they can't invest or plan long term. They tend to be low-key, conservative, and cultivate connections in places of power, for these are the only short-term guarantees of safety.[22]

It's possible that the emerging business class of devout Muslims may help temper extremism in Muslim-majority nations, but can the rise of a religiously conservative bourgeoisie make up for the glaring lack of intellectual freedom in such societies? Scholars like Vali Nasr believe that the power of commerce and Shari´a-compliant financial products could uplift the economies of Muslim-majority nations.[23] By Nasr's accounting, there is a lot of money in the Islamic world. Only five Muslim-majority nations—Egypt, Iran, Pakistan, Saudi Arabia, and Turkey—had a GDP ($3.3 trillion) that was comparable to India's in 2008, although these Muslim nations had only one-third of India's population. Nasr thinks that after Kemalism and fundamentalism, the time for pluralism has arrived. But what he means by this is that Muslims may be willing to live with different forms of Islamic practice, not coexist with non-Muslim beliefs! He does acknowledge in passing that the new Muslim middle class can be "prudish and misogynist,"[24] but he still bets on the power of commerce to liberalize social mores. "Over time," he says, "the profit motive will be our strongest ally." The proposition that capitalism is the answer to religious fundamentalism is a tenuous one, for there are a great many American capitalists, Christian and Jewish alike, who are heavily invested in fundamentalist causes. Nasr's "Shopping Cure," as the *New York Times Book Review* titled its review of the book, doesn't sound enough of a remedy.

That was precisely the point of David Gardner, chief lead writer and associate editor at the *Financial Times*.[25] Having covered the Middle East in the second half of the 1990s and won a prize for his coverage of the Arab world, he knows that what Muslim-majority Arab nations need first and foremost is political reform, not economic change. To Gardner, the argument that the economy may set things right is "crudely determinist, when not downright evasive."[26] There is simply no evidence that economic liberalization could shake up authoritarian regimes. He does, however, agree with Nasr that Turkey's Islamic equivalent of Christian democracy, practiced by Justice and Development, may be the model for a political approach.

Many people see Turkey as a model for the blending of democracy, modernization, and Islam into a workable system, but Turkey's success in blending modernity and faith could not have happened if the country had not undergone an earthshaking transformation led by the uncompromisingly secular leader, Mustafa Kemal. The latter fought for the nation's independence and pursued a comprehensive agenda of social reform that created the structure of today's modern democratic society. He may have been excessive in the way the French Revolution, or even the American Revolution, were; but such revolutions are often necessary to upend centuries of stagnation, despotism, and other social ills. If Turkey's Islamists are in power today, they have their boogeyman Ataturk and modern Europeans to be grateful to, not the Ottoman sultans who ruined their empire by turning their backs on modernity. If there is any doubt about the decadence of the Ottoman Empire, the massive robes worn by the sultans displayed at the Topkapi Palace in Istanbul provide enough evidence of the decay of the Ottoman social body.

I am convinced that the condition of the Muslim-majority nations will not change much if Muslims don't open their minds up and start thinking and believing freely. Perhaps the revolutions that swept across the Arab world could infuse an element of hope in such societies and give us a workable roadmap to the future; but, by the time spring of 2011 turned into summer, it was the Islamist agenda that was asserting its voice. It is ironic, and rather sad, to know that almost two-and-a-half centuries after the American Revolution, the image Americans had of Islam—a religion that fosters tyranny, fanaticism, and slavish behaviors—still prevails in most Muslim-majority nations. Muslims often protest that this has nothing to do with Islam and a lot to do with politics and other conditions. Even if this is true, the fact still remains that Muslims, as a whole, are lagging behind the great advances of our contemporary civilization.

But how can Europe and the United States help produce conditions of freedom in the Islamic world without resorting to destructive misadventures of regime change or the unproductive attitudes of cultural arrogance? Will Turkey drift toward more of the sacred if the European Union keeps blocking its membership? Who can honestly say that Turkey is not part of the European heritage when the country was home to the main events that shaped ancient Mediterranean civilizations, including Christianity? Turkey has a lot to offer Europe and the West. When European economies were mired in debt, recessions, and anemic growth in 2010, Turkey's was growing at the stunning rate of 11.4 percent, the second-largest expansion in the world after China. Having been rejected by the European Union, it turned eastward and found a lot of lucrative business. So successful and robust the country appeared that serious people were wondering whether it was Europe that needed Turkey, not the reverse.[27]

America can be more of an inspiration to Muslims, but not if it doesn't reexamine its assumptions and adapt its revolutionary promise to a fast-changing world. For Muslims to be inspired by the best ideals of America, Americans themselves must show that they care about them. As Gardner said about the West as a whole, "There is no reason for anyone to take our values seriously unless we do."[28] The chairman of the Joint Chiefs of Staff, Adm. Mike Mullen, was even more direct when, in late August 2009, he stated that "each time we fail to live up to our values or don't follow up on a promise, we look more and more like the arrogant Americans the enemy claims we are." The admiral wanted America to be true to its principles and engage Muslims without condescension. "Only through a shared appreciation of the people's culture, needs, and hopes for the future," he wrote, "can we hope ourselves to supplant the extremist narrative."[29]

America's long-held view of Islam as a retrograde, decadent, and fraudulent religion that fosters tyranny and ruin may have been justified by aspects of Muslim history, but Americans could treat Muslims the same way they deal with Europeans today. The American Revolution was not merely the triumph of the new American way of life over Islam, but the overcoming of Europe's failed religions and regimes. American poets invited the whole world to rejoice in the new world order—*novus ordo seclorum*—ushered in by the Revolution. Feudal Europe was a relic of the past and the Catholic Church a satanic institution no better than Islam, really. The United States no longer holds these views of both entities, which means it can do the same with Muslim-majority nations. The light of America guided nations not because early colonists thought they owned the Promised Land, or that they lived in a New Israel or a New Zion, but because the spirit of freedom that inspired the American Revolution was daring and humble, local and global. And its legacy was felt long after the events that gave it rise.

In my next and final chapter, I will make the case that this is the time for all concerned to rediscover the Enlightenment traditions that inspired America's Founding Fathers. Muslims need to liberate themselves from the tyranny of the sacred and approach their beliefs without delusions, while Americans have an obligation to recover their revolutionary heritage and not be driven by short-sighted pecuniary interests. As part of this reconciliation process, all parties involved (American Protestants and Muslims, Israelis and Palestinians) will be prodded to move beyond their millennial myths and overcome their grievances to build a better society for both their peoples. These are all daunting challenges, but America's founders, like Thomas Jefferson, could still provide roadmaps that might help.

Chapter 6

Future without Prejudice

Today's political world is made in the image of the United States. When America's Founding Fathers were drafting the Declaration of Independence, they were acutely aware that they were part of a global economic system. The direct cause of the uprising was tea imported from India through the East India Trading Company. The document itself—the Declaration—was printed by an Irish immigrant on Dutch paper, signed by nine foreign-born colonists with Mexican or Peruvian ink, and addressed to "the Opinions of Mankind." Almost fifty years after he drafted it, Thomas Jefferson affirmed that it was "an appeal to the tribunal of the world was deemed proper for our justification," implying, perhaps, that such global awareness was "intended to be an expression of the American mind." The Declaration was not a call for isolationism or jingoism; it was, as the scholar David Armitage stated, more accurately "a declaration of interdependence."[1] Or, as the historian James Field put it in quintessential literary flair, "secession from the European political system did not involve secession from the human race."[2]

Secede from Europe, though, Americans did. By virtue of acting on the European ideas of the Enlightenment and blending them with America's millennial impulse, the new republic turned into "God's American Israel," in the words of Ezra Stiles, president of Yale, one that is safely removed from the defiling corruption of the Old World. Feudal Europe, with its "Serfs, villains, vassals, noble kings, and gods/All slaves of different grades," wrote the bard of the American Revolution, Joel Barlow, is no match to the United States. "Look not to Europe for examples just/Of order, manners, customs, doctrines, laws, . . . /Thrice wretched lands! Where wealth and splendour glow,/ And want, and misery, in dire contrast show," echoed Barlow's contemporary, Timothy Dwight. America's "Reasoning Race" of fair traders and humanitarian applied scientists, were, in fact, destined to set the people of the world free.[3]

In any case, the Declaration spread around the world like wildfire and has inaugurated "a genre of political writing that has persisted to the present day." It emboldened nations to seek their own independence along the same principles Americans enunciated in the eighteenth century. Today, more than half the world's countries (more than one hundred), inspired by Jefferson's document, have their own declarations of independence. The nation of Czechoslovakia had its own 1918 Declaration drafted in Washington, D.C.; Vietnam's Ho Chi Minh's Declaration (1945) is almost a verbatim copy of the American one.[4] Israel and the United Nations have their own declarations.

Americans and foreigners knew the political significance of the document when it was published. The universal appeal of the United States' founding document—the first to associate "external sovereignty . . . with independence"[5]—was immediately felt. In 1783, Ezra Stiles announced a new era in human knowledge:

> This great American revolution, this recent political phenomenon of a new sovereignty arising among the sovereign powers of the earth, will be attended to and contemplated by all nations. Navigation will carry the American flag around the globe itself; and display the Thirteen Stripes and New Constellation at Bengal and *Canton*, on the Indus and the *Ganaes*, on the *Whana-ho* and the *Yang-tse-kiang* . . . knowledge will be brought home and treasured to *America*; and being here digested and carried to the highest perfection, may reblaze back from *America* to *Europe*, *Asia* and *Africa*, and illumine the world with TRUTH and LIBERTY.[6]

Foreign luminaries agreed. Like many French *philosophes*, Turgot, the great French economist of the period, read in the promise of the American Revolution the birth of the heavenly city that had been anticipated. "It is perhaps in America that the Human race is to be recreated; that it is to adopt a new and sublime legislation, that it is to perfect the arts and sciences, that it is to recreate the nations of antiquity. America is the asylum of liberty . . . and will prove what man can do when he adds to knowledge a courageous heart."[7] In 1786, five years after Turgot's death, and a decade after the Declaration was issued, another great French economist Nicolas de Condorcet declared that

[i]t is not enough that the rights of man be written in the books of philosophers and the hearts of virtuous men; the ignorant and weak man must be able to read them in the example of a great people. America has given us this example. The act that declared American independence is a simple and sublime statement of these sacred and long-forgotten rights."[8]

The following year, the French royal censor Abbé Genty expressed even more enthusiasm: "The independence of Anglo-Americans is the event most likely to accelerate the revolution that must bring happiness on earth. . . . In the bosom of this new republic are the true treasures that will enrich the world."[9] That the American Revolution inaugurated "a new era in the history of the world" was acknowledged even by European antirevolutionaries like Schmidt-Phiseldek.[10]

Just before Jefferson died in 1826, around twenty Declarations had already been signed by other nations.[11] That year the United States was celebrating its fiftieth anniversary, so, quite appropriately, Jefferson wrote a public letter reflecting on the significance of the Declaration, describing it as "an instrument, pregnant with our own and the fate of the world."[12] He added:

May it be to the world, what I believe it will be—to some parts sooner, to others later, but finally to all—the signal of arousing men to burst the chains under which monkish ignorance and superstition had persuaded them to bind themselves, and to assume the blessings and security of self-government. That form (of government) which we have substituted, restores the free right to the unbounded exercise of reason and freedom of opinion. All eyes are opened, or opening, to the rights of man. The general spread of the light of science has already laid open to every view the palpable truth, that the mass of mankind has not been born with saddles on their backs, nor a favored few booted and spurred, ready to ride them legitimately, by the grace of God. These are grounds of hope for others. For ourselves, let the annual return of this day forever refresh our recollections of these rights, and an undiminished devotion to them.

Abraham Lincoln knew that the Declaration would be the single most powerful invention of the United States when he paid tribute to its main author: "All honor to Jefferson," he declared, "to the man who, in the concrete pressure of a struggle for national independence by a single people, had the coolness, forecast, capacity to introduce into a merely revolutionary document, an abstract truth, applicable to all men and all time."[13]

The new American nation, the "ark of liberties," as Herman Melville, and more recently, Ted Widmer, described it, emerged as "the most successful new nation in history."[14] When John L. O'Sullivan, the Irish Catholic immigrant who, in 1845, coined the phrase that came to embody America's new role on the world stage—"manifest destiny"—he was thinking of the United States as a messenger of freedom. In an essay published in late 1839, the journalist who was born near Gibraltar, educated in England and France, and started out as an anti-imperialist committed to social justice, described his country as "The Great Nation of Futurity":

> Our national birth was the beginning of a new history, the formation and progress of an untried political system, which separates us from the past and connects us with the future only; and so far as regards the entire development of the natural rights of man, in moral, political and national life, we may confidently assume that our country is destined to be the great nation of futurity. . . . The far-reaching, the boundless future will be the era of American greatness. In its magnificent domain of space and time, the nation of many nations is destined to manifest to mankind the excellence of divine principles; to establish on earth the noblest temple ever dedicated to the worship of the Most High—the Sacred and the True. Its floor shall be a hemisphere—its roof the firmament of the star-studded heavens, and its congregation an Union of many Republics, comprising hundreds of happy millions, calling, owning no man master, but governed by God's natural and moral law of equality, the law of brotherhood—of "peace and good will amongst men."[15]

But what O'Sullivan later termed America's "manifest destiny," as noble as the concept had initially been, turned out to be a convenient ideology in the hands of racial supremacists and warmongers. Albert Gallatin, a Swiss immigrant who sailed to America to fight on behalf of the Revolution, was still alive when the United States unjustly invaded Mexico. In 1847, he, like George Washington in his 1796 farewell address, warned against the perversions of patriotism.[16]

Dreams of a world made in the image of the United States were not uncommon, but the American model was not quite sorted out, as slavery, racism, and xenophobia continued to threaten the promise of the republic. Manifest destiny, even in the hands of its initial promoter, was acquiring the reddish hues of colonial violence inflicted on others. All these developments worried Abraham Lincoln. In an 1855 letter, he wrote:

> Our progress in degeneracy appears to me to be pretty rapid. As a nation, we began by declaring that, "all men are created equal." We now practically read it "all men are created equal, except Negroes." When the Know-Nothings get control, it will read "all men are created equal, except negroes, and foreigners, and catholics." When it comes to this I should prefer emigrating to some country where they make no pretense of loving liberty—to Russia, for instance, where despotism can be taken pure, and without the base alloy of hypocracy [hypocrisy].[17]

Still, the notion of the United States as a chosen nation with a providential mission persisted. President Woodrow Wilson, who shaped the modern world of politics in profound ways, was a believer. When he introduced himself to the American people in 1912, he told them that "we are chosen, and prominently chosen to show the way to the nations of the world how they shall walk in the path of liberty."[18] In 1913, he publicly vowed not to encroach on anyone's territory and, as we have seen earlier, refrained from declaring war on Turkey, which was on the side of Germany, out of respect for the long history of missionary work in that country. In this way, the United States maintained its friendly disposition toward the people of the Middle East, which made it, as Kemal Ataturk would say, "more acceptable than the rest."[19] When Wilson proposed his Fourteen Points after the War and arrived in France for the Versailles negotiations, he was hailed in the streets of Paris an American savior, the "God of Peace," or the "Moses from Across the Atlantic." He championed the League of Nations. Until he succumbed to a stroke in 1919, he remained a fervent believer in the American people's commitment to justice and liberty.[20]

This American legacy survived in the vision and wisdom of Franklin D. Roosevelt. In his famous "Four Freedoms" address to Congress on January 6, 1941, he declared that the world he envisions is attainable in his generation. Over the next few years and until his death, his call for a set of human rights for the American people remained steadfast.[21] He also wanted the same for the world's oppressed and colonized people, those who resent being ruled by

what he called a "handful of whites." He knew that European colonialism was making a potential enemy of more than one billion people.[22] Like Wilson, he was behind the creation of the United Nations.
He was highly respected in the Islamic world, holding major summits
in Casablanca, Cairo, and Teheran. He even had plans to spend two
years in the Middle East to help bring the desert back to life through
modern forestry and agricultural techniques. His wife Eleanor was
at the head of the committee drafting the Universal Declaration of
Human Rights, a document that borrows from the US Declaration; so
was Charles Malik, an alumnus of the American University of Beirut
that American missionaries established in the nineteenth century.[23]

The United States remained highly admired during the Cold War.
Through the Marshall Plan, it helped Europe get back on its feet
after a devastating war. As I suggested above, the Vietnamese Ho
Chi Minh was so inspired by the US Declaration and the nation's
revolutionary traditions that he wrote Vietnam's own Declaration
of Independence and read it to a huge crowd on September 2, 1945.
Pan-Africanist Kwame Nkrumah's "Motion of Destiny" in 1953
echoed Winthrop's sermon: "The eyes and ears of the world are
upon you; yea, our oppressed brothers throughout the vast continent
of Africa and the New World are looking to you with desperate
hope." On April 18, 1953, the Indonesian president Sukarno coined
the term "third world" on the anniversary of the day Paul Revere
rode to Concord in 1775 and sparked "the first anti-colonialist war
in history."[24]

By the 1950s, the United States took a rather un-American turn
and started making more enemies, rather than inspiring admirers.
With right-wing paranoia and anti-Communism driving policies at
home and abroad, the United States chose to undermine Iran's democratic process and impose one of the worst dictators of the twentieth
century on that country's people. Eager to claim a fairer portion of
the revenue of the oil exploited by the Anglo-Iranian Oil Company
(the forerunner of BP, the company that spoiled the US Gulf Coast
in 2010), Iranians had elected the highly respected member of parliament, Mohammed Mossadegh, in 1951. This was such a great event
that *Time* magazine chose Mossadegh as its Man of the Year. In the
next two years, Iranians lived in a climate of political democracy.
But the newly created Central Intelligence Agency (CIA) convinced
by the British that Mossadegh was too weak to resist Soviet Communism, orchestrated a coup against the man who was popularly

elected and deposed him in 1953. The huge consequences of this event have remained with us ever since. As Stephen Kinzer wrote, "For a nearly a century, Iranians had known America's benevolent side. Thousands had attended American schools or been treated at the American Hospital of Tehran. Howard Baskerville and Morgan Schuster were national heroes. This golden age was about to end."[25]

The overthrow of Mossadegh would become a template for the overthrow of Latin American regimes. As US military bases proliferated overseas, President Eisenhower warned in 1961 his fellow citizens about the threat to American democracy of the "military-industrial complex." In 1957, John F. Kennedy had argued that the Cold War was distorting American foreign policy and made the case for Algerian freedom fighters, sometimes dismissed as "terrorists," because they were fighting for their independence. He even wanted the United States to support independence movements around the world—an unusual position to take at that time.[26] It was, however, left to Jimmy Carter to deal with the blowback resulting from the 1953 coup against Mossadegh and the human rights abuses of the pro-American shah who replaced him.

In its 1975 report, Amnesty International concluded that "no country in the world has a worse human rights record than Iran";[27] yet such a damning report had no significant impact even on a president who made human rights his signature policy. It took the United States almost fifty years to acknowledge its terrible mistake toward Iran. On March 17, 2000, Secretary of State Madeleine Albright told the American Iranian Council:

> In 1953 the United States played a significant role in orchestrating the overthrow of Iran's popular Prime Minister, Mohammed Mossadegh. The Eisenhower Administration believed its actions were justified for strategic reasons; but the coup was dearly a setback for Iran's political development. And it's easy to see now why many Iranians continue to resent this intervention by America in their internal affairs.
>
> Moreover, during the next quarter-century, the United States and the West gave sustained backing to the Shah's regime. Although it did much to develop the country economically, the Shah's government also brutally repressed political dissent.[28]

This and subsequent US policies toward Iran were deemed "short-sighted," a fact that President Obama reiterated in 2009; but has the United States repaired its vision vis-à-vis Iran or the Islamic world as a whole? Following the barbaric attacks on the United States on September 11, 2001, Iranians spontaneously walked out in demonstrations to express solidarity with the country that was soon to be labeled a member of the axis of evil.[29] Of course, the theocratic regime in Iran doesn't inspire hope for the future, with medieval Islamic law still imposed on a sophisticated nation of artists, filmmakers, scientists, and scholars. But threatening Iran only causes the regime to barricade itself behind more rigid measures. Iranians, as they did in the first decade of the twentieth century and again in 1951, are still yearning for democracy, but threats are not helping liberalize their society. Twice in the course of the twentieth century the Iranians' aspirations for democracy and freedom were thwarted by Western powers, so why should the Iranians trust the United States if it continues to display belligerent intent?

Remember when I mentioned in the introduction ("Why America Matters") that Truman sent the USS *Missouri* with the remains of Turkey's ambassador in 1946? Turkey had long admired the American republic. Americans helped it rebuild its navy in the nineteenth century and founded important educational institutions for its people. In the twentieth century, Turkey opened its doors to US servicemen and gave American sailors anything they wanted. Turkish soldiers fought side by side with their American comrades in Korea. But during the Vietnam War in the 1960s, Turkish hospitality started to turn into anger, as the United States became more visible through its thousands of servicemen on Turkish soil than for any gestures of goodwill. By the time the aircraft carrier USS *Forrestal* came to Istanbul in 1969, sailors were greeted with protests and women displaying signs saying "Istanbul Is Not a Brothel for the Sixth Fleet."[30] So much had changed in a mere two decades!

Even the US economic system is in question today as a model for Muslims, or the globe, for that matter. William Greider, the longtime economic observer of the United States, thinks that Americans are in for a painful readjustment because gross disparities in wealth are tearing apart the legacy that the Founding Fathers left to the nation and the world. If revolutionary Americans despised the feudal order in Europe with its vast social inequalities, the United States seems to have switched places with its old nemesis. As the nation slips from what used to be its undisputed first rank in the global economy, the rich are drowning in a consumer culture of superabundance, while increasing parts of the country are beginning to look like failed states. While a sprawling "military-industrial complex" siphons off increasingly scarce resources for dubious military adventures in the Middle East and elsewhere, the national infrastructure and other badly need social investments, such as education, are left to fend for themselves. Greider has some very good suggestions on how to revitalize the American promise at home,[31] but I will only note here that a vibrant American economy, one that is equitable and sustainable, is a far better approach for global leadership than a permanent quest for armament.

Currently, neither the dominant economic paradigm, nor a traditional relationship to Muslim-majority nations, will restore America's traditional leadership and dispel the cloud of pessimism that has hovered over the nation in the last few years. Just like the Muslim-majority nations have to rethink their relationship to traditions and the world they live in, so does the United States have to reevaluate its own assumptions and place in the world today, particularly with the Islamic world. As Abraham Lincoln, who revered the Declaration of Independence, stated in 1862, when the Civil War was in full swing, "The dogmas of the quiet past are inadequate to the stormy present. . . . As our case is new, so we must think anew, and act anew."[32]

Appealing to the "Opinions of Mankind," as Thomas Jefferson and his fellow Founding Fathers did, is still the surest way to regain the world's affections and renew America's leadership in the world. The United States has produced mesmerizing forms of entertainment, a cornucopia of consumer goods that would have made the Ottoman sultans of old envious, and arms that could annihilate any rival, but it is neglecting to promote the very best thing it has ever produced—the language of freedom and justice embedded in its Declaration of Independence. This document embodies the spirit of America itself, yet its ideals and principles have been left to languish while the brute forces of might and power are running roughshod over its future and the future of world civilization. There has never been a better time for Americans, and the world, to rediscover America's revolutionary heritage. President Obama's support of democracy-seeking protesters during the Arab Spring of 2011 was a good first step because it repositioned the United States on the side of the long-oppressed Muslim people, not their repressive governments. As I explained earlier in this book, the Arab uprisings were justified in light of the dispatches on Arab corrupt regimes by

US diplomats (brought to light by WikiLeaks) and quietly enabled and supported by the US government and American companies like Google and Facebook. Although the US intervention in Libya could be seen as yet another example of America's insatiable quest for war and a waste of America's dwindling financial commitments, many in Libya saw it a liberating act, one that was wholeheartedly welcomed by most Libyan anti-Qaddafi rebels. But the United States needs to do more to reclaim the trust and admiration of Muslims and Arabs. Foregrounding America's progressive spirit will have to guide not just one administration or party, but the entire political system—in fact, the whole nation needs to be mobilized in this effort, if only to renew its own commitment to the Revolution.

Once America's spirit is reignited, it would be much easier to address Muslims convincingly. If America's old Puritans and today's evangelicals continue to read Islam through the lenses of Old Testament prophecies, then it is incumbent upon all peace-seeking, cultured Americans to question and counter such beliefs vigorously. The United States, unlike most nations of the West, is closest to Muslim societies when it comes to religion, and so must make a similar effort at deploying reason against the tales and prophecies of scripture. And if such changes turn out to be daunting, then a new, supernatural villain needs to replace the Muslim Antichrist, just like the Catholics have ceded that honor to the Russians before. Perhaps Hollywood can invent an enemy we can all hate!

Catholics were once satanic in the Protestant moral order, but that enmity has been mended by merging all believers under the canopy of mere Christianity. Jews were a fallen lot to be converted, but they, too, have been included. In this fashion, Protestant America became a Judeo-Christian nation. As a monotheistic religion that shares much with both faiths, especially Judaism, Islam could also be integrated into a larger ecumenical doctrine. Since religions are designed for social cohesion, there is no reason not to imagine a more capacious faith for monotheistically inclined Americans. The country would be much better off getting closer to the deism of Jefferson and other Founding Fathers, but given the high rates of religiosity in the country, it is doubtful whether such prospect can be expected in the near future.

The United States kept Europe at arms' length during its inception, but now transatlantic trade and relations are the best they have ever been. The United States' relations with its old foes, in other words, have turned into an amicable and enriching exchange. This happened because both entities—the United States and Europe—changed over the course of the last two centuries. And so by helping Muslims change, the United States could find in the Islamic world a better and more engaging partner. If twenty-first-century Americans could lend the same helping hand that guided missionaries in the nineteenth, they would be doing Muslims and themselves much good. The goal, of course, is not to convert, but to educate. The gospel of education is a far more powerful tool than any weapon in the US arsenal. Muslims and Arabs are still coveting American higher education, even if they object to US politics. Oil-rich Arab states are in a rush to buy the best of America's private higher education, but the US government could reach out to the poor and struggling middle classes, the social groups that gravitate toward extremism, and help provide good education and other social services, including sports fields and libraries stocked with good books and copies of the Declaration and other materials that showcase the grandeur of the American nation. It could reopen the popular and iconic American Cultural Centers, whose number fell from more than three hundred in the early 1970s to a mere thirty-nine in 2011.[33]

Following the toppling of Egyptian president Hosni Mubarak in February 2011, the Egyptian American Nobel Prize laureate in chemistry Ahmed Zewail told the *New York Times* columnist Thomas Friedman that "nothing would have a bigger impact" on Egypt than using some of the money allocated to Egypt's military support to build ten world-class schools across the country. Friedman went further: writing a few weeks later, the columnist convincingly argued that diverting some of the 110 billion dollars the US government futilely lavishes on Pakistan and Afghanistan to counter Islamic extremism would be far better spent on the fledgling Arab democracies, helping them to relieve some of their debt and providing them with scholarships to US universities.[34]

If the United States is to engage in propaganda, it can't do better than telling its own story. Mike Mullen, the Chairman of the Joint Chiefs of Staff, said as much in 2009 when he reminded us that the United States is always at its best when it acts on its ideals, as it did, for example, when it helped Europe recover from its devastating destruction with the Marshall Plan after World War II. As was the case of social missionaries in Arab lands in the nineteenth century, what was good for Americans was also good for other people.

Along with this outreach, and armed with a new ecumenical faith that includes Islam, the United States could then renegotiate its commitments with all Muslim-majority nations and tackle the Israeli-Palestinian question with renewed vigor. The problem is by now too complicated to be approached with the lenses of a black-and-white morality tale. In 1906, the Christian promoter of Arab nationalism Najib Azouri could predict that Arab and Jewish nationalisms were destined to fight it out over Palestine and that the fate of the world would depend on the outcome of this existential clash. In 1931, Ameen Rihani, the great champion of American values mentioned in my previous chapter, knew that world peace depended on a peaceful solution in Palestine. "The cradle of the Prince of Peace," he wrote, "is still today as it was in the past, a victim of Satanic humor."[35] Writing before Israel came into existence, Rihani feared that without a fair resolution for local Arabs, the Palestinian issue could inflame the Muslim world against the West—although, at that time, he was thinking of a Muslim revolt against European colonial powers. To Rihani, it was the British who played roulette with the fate of Palestine, making separate pledges for support to Arabs and Jews and dividing two people who had long lived together in relative peace.[36]

Azouri and Rihani's predictions and warnings have turned out to be true. Muslims the world over remain deeply disillusioned over Israel's heavy-handed treatment of the Palestinians as well as the inability of Israel's main international sponsor (the United States) to intervene forcefully and fairly in the long dispute. This is an understandable expectation, but Muslims and Arabs would also have to accept that their states, like the state of Israel, are new creations; and if Israel was born through indomitable will and might at the expense of local Palestinians, few states in the world today could claim nobler births. The United States certainly has a lot to atone for with its Native populations. In fact, the entire American continent is built on the blood of indigenous people who perished a century or so after Columbus landed in the New World. As tragic and inhumane as the fate of Native Americans is, we simply can't imagine removing Mexico, Venezuela, Chile, or Brazil from the political map of the world.

The same applies to Muslim-majority nations. If Muslims hadn't invaded Anatolia and toppled Constantinople, Turkey would not exist as a Muslim nation. Iran would not be Muslim today if the

Persian Sassanid Empire had not been overthrown by Arabs. Christians would not have launched crusades against Muslims in the Middle Ages if Muslims had not taken over Christian lands in the Middle East and Spain. North Africa would not be part of the Arab League if Arabs hadn't galloped through its lands and forced the native Berbers to convert to Islam. Algeria would not exist in its present form if the French had not carved out its borders from neighboring countries. The truth is that political geographies have never been stable. This is, unfortunately, the story of the world. Some nations come into existence, some vanish, and others go through mutations, changing shapes and sizes as they hang on to their place on the map.

The United States could nudge Israel and Palestine to find a solution through a sober analysis of history. Until the modern period, Jews and Muslims lived in an enriching symbiotic relationship, despite the constraints of religious zeal and the humiliations Jews were forced to endure as minorities throughout the Islamic world. To be sure, Jews did far better in Muslim lands than they did in Christendom, but the Jews' legal status as second-class citizens (*dhimmis*) made them easy targets for persecution, harassment, forced conversions, and even pogroms. Martin Gilbert's recent account of Jews in Islamic countries provides abundant documentation of the bloodcurdling horrors visited upon them, even in lands (such as Egypt and Iraq) where they had lived long before Islam appeared in Arabia.[37]

I remember all too well the social denigration of Jews in my native Tangier. When I was growing up in the 1960s and 1970s, calling someone a Jew was an insult—it meant being cheap and devious, as if these were the fundamental characteristics of the Jewish people. I cared deeply about the plight of the Palestinians, whose travails were chronicled daily in our media, but I knew nothing about the history of my Jewish neighbors. In fact, it was my exposure to America that helped me see past my prejudices. Soon after I came to New York to study in 1983, I was walking with a fellow Tangerian, a nice young man who had invited me to his wedding in Connecticut, and, in the process of chatting, I referred to someone as a Jew, in the derogatory sense mentioned above. My friend gently informed me that his mother was Jewish, and, in order to make me comfortable, added that she had converted to Islam. I later visited my friend's kind mother in Tangier with a deep sense of humility and guilt, but the episode was a stark reminder of how easy it is to imbibe one's cultural prejudices and how difficult it is to become aware of them, let alone contest them publicly. I have been biting my cultural lip ever since. If I, from liberal Tangier, could speak like that, I can only imagine what more zealous Muslims in less cosmopolitan settings might think.

It is time for Jews and Muslims, Israelis and Palestinians to see past their prejudices and strike a new friendship, one based on equality, not tolerance. Muslims have a lot to learn from their political adversaries. Israel may, in fact, be the closet model they have in thinking about how to build a future of cultural and political freedoms while giving due respect to religion.

With its never-ending tensions around the place of biblical edicts in a secular state, Israel is a laboratory for the creation and maintenance of a religiously imprinted democratic system. Israel fares far better than Muslim countries because of the social and political freedoms its citizens enjoy, although, like Iran, Pakistan, or Saudi Arabia, it still has to work out the contradiction of promoting democracy while insisting on the Jewish character of its nation. If Israel manages to retain its Jewish memory while making its society a democracy without exceptions, Islamic nations would certainly have no excuse not to do the same. (It would, however, be most ironic if Israel turned its Arab citizens in its midst into a new version of *dhimmis*.)

In fact, even when it comes to the quarrel between Jews and Arabs, the latter are more likely to find support in Israel than they do in the United States. Israeli rabbis, historians, and human rights activists have all stood up for Palestinian villagers against the various injustices committed against them, whether by settlers or by the Israeli government. Palestinian prisoners are treated far more humanely in Israeli prisons than they are in Palestinian jails. Muslims who have access to Israeli television are sometimes treated to the spectacle of Israeli Arabs in the Knesset condemning Israeli policies with impunity, a freedom that most Muslims don't have in their own "free" countries.[38] And if Muslims think that Israel is a European body in their Oriental midst, it is not quite right to think of Jews as colonizers in the same way the French were in Algeria. Jews had been dreaming of rebuilding their temple since it was destroyed for the second time in 70 A.D., almost six centuries before Islam was born in the Arabian Peninsula. And when they started mobilizing to go back, many of them thought of themselves as Orientals, not Westerners.

Indeed, a good number of nineteenth-century prominent Jews identified so completely with the Islamic heritage that they expressed contempt for the upstart civilization of Europe. (German Jews today continue to stand up for Muslims and their cultural rights.)[39] If we accept the German classification of Semitism, then Jews, genetically and religiously, must be considered long-lost Middle Easterners returning home with new knowledge to build stronger societies. Despite discrimination against Jews from Muslim lands in Israel, Israelis from advanced Western societies are, in an ironic way, reversing the region's brain drain and bringing with them the tools for a great take off for the entire region.

As early as 1906, the Arab author Farid Kassab didn't hesitate to tell his audience that Jews were at home in Palestine and that Jewish settlers have revitalized agriculture and industry and, therefore, rendered an "immense service to the country."[40] In 1919, Emir Feisal, the leader of the Arab revolt against the Ottomans, signed an agreement with Dr. Chaim Weizeman, the leader of the Zionist movement, affirming the "the racial kinship and ancient bonds existing between the Arabs and the Jewish people"[41] and welcoming the Jews to their historic land in Palestine. Later that year, Feisal wrote a letter to the American Zionist Felix Frankfurter reaffirming that "Arabs and Jews are cousins, having suffered similar oppressions at the hands of powers stronger than themselves, and by a happy coincidence have been able to take the first step toward the attainment of their national ideals together."[42] Feisal added that "the Jewish movement is national and not imperialistic" and that both Jews and Arabs need each other to uplift both peoples. When Feisal was proclaimed king in 1921, he was honored by Jewish poets in Baghdad and given a precious copy of the Pentateuch. Sixteen years later, after the British had recommended partition in 1937, David Ben-Gurion echoed the same sentiments when he told members of the British Peel Commission that Jews and Arabs could "benefit each other" and that a free Jewish nation in Palestine could spur the kind of collaboration that would be the basis of peace and prosperity. In fact, the idea of a new Jewish state being beneficial to its neighbors had been a staple of both Christian and Jewish Zionist thinking. It is stated in Theodor Herzl's *The Jewish State* (1896) and Israel's Declaration of Independence (1948).[43]

If only Ben-Gurion's wish had come to pass! In its short existence as a state, Israel has emerged as a superpower in agricultural technological innovations, relying on the egalitarian spirit inculcated in most of its citizens through universal military service, the *chutzpah* of its people, the irrepressible penchant of its entrepreneurs for start-ups, and its first-class educational system (parts of which were established long before the state itself was founded) to attract investors and sell its products globally. When Salom Rizk, the "Syrian Yankee," was on his way to the Middle East after a six-year sojourn in America, he shared a cabin with European Jews fleeing the Nazis to Palestine and wondered how they could possibly prosper in a land without resources. But a Jewish professor from Boston University told him that Jews "don't need opportunities. They make opportunities." Later, Rizk wrote in his diary that such exiles may, in fact, be carrying with them "a hint of international hope."[44]

By developing the technique of drip irrigation in the 1960s and being the world leader in recycling wastewater, Israel has reversed desertification, grown forests on the Negev Desert, and turned the lands once described by Mark Twain and other nineteenth-century travelers as desolate into one of the most prosperous nations in the world. Israel today is an agricultural powerhouse, producing almost all of the food it needs and offsets the cost of imported foods with its own agricultural exports. Such plenitude is even more striking when we learn that the nation puts no restrictions on Jewish immigration and hosts more than seventy different nationalities. Not only that, Israel is so committed to babies that it is the only country in the world that subsidizes in vitro fertilization for couples who can't conceive naturally, and it does so for Jewish and Arab citizens without distinction. Israel has been able to do this because it encourages critical thinking that verges on insubordination, even in the military. Unlike Dubai and other oil-rich Arab states, Israel produces its world-class scientists and ideas; it doesn't just import them.[45]

The whole world, including Muslims, have benefited from Israeli inventions and expertise. And Muslims could benefit more if a just peace could be reached. For example, in the summer of 2010, Professor David Levy, from the Faculty of Agriculture of the Hebrew University of Jerusalem (founded in 1918), developed a potato that could grow in extreme weather and be irrigated with salt water. That same year, an Israeli company developed a tomato that could withstand room temperature for a week and still retain its firmness and freshness.[46] Since most Arab countries are water-starved and very warm, they stand to benefit greatly from such groundbreaking agricultural innovations.

I am not a Palestinian who has experienced the trauma of dislocation, so I can only imagine the intensity of the Palestinians' grievances and the depth of their humiliation as they huddle precariously in ghetto-like settings or in foreign countries, longing to reclaim their confiscated homes and lands. The Palestinians' pain is real, not abstract. But as painful as the Israelis' policies are to the Palestinians, history cannot be undone. We have a better chance at shaping the course of the future, but we can't change the past. If peace is done right and the region were to merge into, say, an open economic and cultural commonwealth, then there is no better thing for Israelis and Palestinians to do right now. Arabs need to learn from the Jewish example if they want to move ahead. It was no less a figure than Constantine Zurayk, the Arab nationalist who coined the term "*nakba*" (catastrophe) to describe the devastating loss of Palestine in 1948, who excoriated his fellow Arabs for being trapped in a "torpid imagination and vague and ruinous romanticism." The Zionists triumphed, he wrote in *The Meaning of the Nakba*, because they embraced a "modern Western life," and did not turn their backs on it. "The reason lies in that they live in the present and for the future," he continued, "whereas we still dream the dreams of the past and stupefy ourselves in its bygone glory."[47]

More than half a century later, an aggrieved Palestinian father whose twenty-year-old son was killed when a Palestinian terrorist mistook him for a Jew, and whose family suffered grievously at the hand of Zionists, paid for the translation of *A Tale of Love and Darkness*, the acclaimed autobiography of Israeli writer Amos Oz, and said: "We can learn from it how a people like the Jewish people emerged from the tragedy of the Holocaust and were able to reorganize themselves and build their country and become an independent people. If we can't learn from that, we will not be able to do anything for our independence."[48] As painful as the Palestinians' injuries might be, Palestinians and their supporters would be doing more harm by not seriously creating conditions of growth and prosperity for the Palestinians' children and grandchildren. A prosperous future in peace is today's Palestinian militant's best revenge. Israel stands to benefit, too, as new, money-drenched markets of oil-rich Arab nations would be open to its technology and products.

Anyone who cares about the prospect of a better future for Israelis and Arabs or Jews and Muslims should challenge any claim to colonization that is based on biblical prophecy and Second Coming scenarios. Israel and Palestine should be conceived as mere states trying to negotiate an acceptable peace settlement that can meet the needs of both people, but investing the disputed land with supernatural powers will only confuse the issue and delay a reasonable outcome. We cannot negotiate with divine decrees and mandates, but we can agree on a political settlement. We need more logical reasoning and less recourse to the sacred. Religious myths may have been the driving force for the creation of Israel, but they may very well be impeding the fusion of Jews and Arabs in one democratic state.

Until the creation of Israel in 1948, Jews had practically no experience governing a state. But now, as Bernard Lewis wrote in 2010, "they have a state, and they are rapidly acquiring a church" and "relations between the two are becoming an issue." Israelis, in other words, are now facing the same fundamental issue confronting Muslims—namely, whether to opt for a secular state or a religious one. Unlike the New Testament, Jewish scripture doesn't divide the realms of sovereignty between Caesar and God, but one could find Jewish rituals in today's Israel (such as the ceremony of the *havdala*) that separate the profane from the sacred. Lewis, therefore, suggests that this may very well be the next step for Israel to take.[49]

Such a step is, in fact, the only way to avoid discrimination against Israel's Arab or Muslim citizens. Using the Bible, the Qur'an, or any other sacred scripture to justify social injustice is simply not a good long-term solution. If a two-state solution is not possible, then there is no logical reason why Jews and Arabs can't share one land, provided all citizens share the same rights and obligations. Even right-wing Israelis are beginning to wonder whether a one-state solution is the only practical option left.[50] Such an approach would not be anti-Zionist in the least because the principle of equal citizenship, regardless of religion or ethnicity, is enshrined in Israel's founding document, the Declaration of Independence. Israel, such document states, "will uphold the full social and political equality of all its citizens without distinction of religion, race, or sex; will guarantee freedom of religion, conscience, education and culture; will safeguard the Holy Places of all religions."[51]

As we have seen earlier in this book, the mania for the Holy Land in the nineteenth century didn't last long; it gave way to disillusionment with the region. The place simply had too much religion. Or, to use the argument of Diner in relation to Muslims, Israelis and Palestinians alike are terrorized by the sacred. Tales of the Bible and the Qur'an have turned ancient buildings into divine artifacts and signs of people's election, as if God blessed only the lands of the Middle East and didn't care much about, say, Norway, Iceland, or Uruguay.

Archaeological evidence has left no doubt that much of the history in the Old Testament—such as the Exodus, the violent conquest of Canaan, and the great reigns of David and his son Solomon—was a figment of the brilliant imagination of writers in the seventh century B.C. Although there is no material proof that a Temple of Solomon, as we imagine it, ever existed, many Christian and religious Zionists are convinced that the Jewish temple, destroyed almost two thousand years ago, must rise on the ruins of the Aqsa mosque and Dome of the Rock in Jerusalem, if prophecy, with its Armageddon scenarios, is to be fulfilled.[52]

In *Hidden Histories: Palestine and the Eastern Mediterranean* (2010), Basem L. Ra'ad, a professor at Al-Quds University in Jerusalem, shows that many of today sacred places were created *ex nihilo*, out of an attempt to impose the one true religion on a pagan, polytheistic environment. As Ra'ad asks, "How could humans know or have remembered where Noah and Joseph were buried, or where the bush of Moses is supposed to have burned? Was it really possible to know the exact spot where Christ [assuming he was a historical figure] was born or entombed?"[53] Sites such as the Ibrahimi Mosque (Al Haram el Ibrahimi) in Hebron, the Nativity Church, the Church of the Holy Sepulcher, the Western/Wailing Wall, Rachel's Tomb, and others were all designated arbitrarily. There is no historical record to prove their sacredness. In fact, it was Emperor Constantine's mother Helena who, through "divine inspiration" in A.D. 323, baptized pagan sites into Christian ones. Thus, a basilica was built on a pagan site and a mosque was built on the remains of basilica on the belief that it rested on Solomon's Temple. The Wailing Wall is most certainly not what's left of the destroyed temple but the remains of a Roman fortress. It was sanctified by Sephardic Jews fleeing Spanish persecution in the sixteenth century. As *The Encyclopedia Judaica* wrote in its 1971 edition: "In the geonic period the place of assembly and prayer for Jews was on the Mount of Olives. The Western Wall became a permanent feature of Jewish tradition about [A.D.] 1520, either as a result of the immigration of the Spanish exiles or in the wake of the Turkish conquest of 1518."[54] Yet this wall is not only assumed to be the remains of the "second" temple, but also that it stands on the same site where the "first" temple of Solomon had been erected. It doesn't matter that by the time of Solomon (tenth century B.C.), there was no Judaism as we know it today. And to complicate matters further, new theories, based on genetic studies, are pointing to the possibility that Palestinians are descendants of Jews who stayed home but were forced to convert.[55]

If the protagonists in this divine drama insist on the holiness of their land, then they should abdicate all quests for secular power and let God handle the whole situation without any human intervention. Another way to look at this, suggested in 2006 by the Slovenian philosopher Slavoj Zizek, is to renounce any political control over the contested parts of Jerusalem.[56] A museum-like neutral space that accommodates clashing religious passions is better than oversight by one religious group of another. For purposes of peace among humans, preserving the sacredness of life is better than adhering to millennia-old prejudices.

After enduring millennia of atrocities, Jews cannot afford not to have a place of their own. The challenge is how to conceive of such a place. One hopes that by the time this book is published, Israelis and Palestinians would have come closer to peaceful coexistence than at any time in the two people's history in the last century. If they haven't, then it is time for both sides to start talking beyond their grievances and toward long-lasting, humane solutions.

Changing deeply rooted patterns in human relationship is never easy. When President Obama addressed the Islamic world from Cairo in 2009 and Jakarta in 2010, he told us that building a new future of cooperation and understanding between the United States and the Islamic world will take time. But Obama's modesty may have prevented him from pointing out to the best of American traditions to inspire change in the Islamic world, and, indeed, in parts of his country. It is the election of Obama in 2008—more than any other event in recent political memory—that vindicates Jefferson's hope in the power of the Declaration. Cultural habits may block change for years or decades, but the winds of freedom that are unleashed by America's founding document have a way of sweeping them aside over time. Only a few decades ago, a man of African descent would not have been admitted into an American restaurant; but in 2008, Americans voted for a politician who, in the words of Middle East scholar Juan Cole, "unites within himself American and African Muslim heritages."[57] If Israel Zangwill, the author of the play *The Melting Pot*, which opened in New York in 1908, called, through his protagonist, the Jewish Russian immigrant David Quixano, the United States, "God's Crucible," it was because all nationalities eventually blend into an American identity.[58] America, it seems, is where Old World ethnicities are recycled into a new world order of common citizens.

America's revolutionary spirit, inspired by the philosophies of the Enlightenment, gave Americans the strength to break away from European political traditions and imagine bold new beginnings for themselves and the world. Men like Thomas Jefferson, Benjamin Franklin, and George Washington knew that religious instincts were very strong among the people they represented and fought for, but they also knew that blind faith in scripture could lead to false worship. They were too ahead of their time to express their views publicly, but Jefferson did downsize the Bible by editing out redundancies and bringing its tales down to earth—Jesus, to him, was a remarkable leader inspired by the noblest of sentiments. That, I imagine, was sacred enough.

Although I agree with Diner that Muslims today seem to be unable to step out of the prison house of the sacred, unexamined Christianity and Judaism will also continue to misguide us politically and culturally if they are not seriously questioned. World leaders, as well as peace makers of all sorts, often ask us to be open to our religious differences and to turn our faiths into instruments of friendship, not pretexts for war. But would it be too radical to say that it is our religions that have kept us apart? The Puritans who landed in America didn't mince words when it came to Islam—to them, it was a fraudulent faith inspired by a debauched pseudo-prophet. This view permeated America's consciousness through the centuries and has remained with us, in one form or another, ever since.

Whether in religious or secular terms, Islam has never had good press in the United States. To be sure, Muslims were given theoretical rights by Thomas Jefferson, but few Americans were impressed by a faith that was Christianity's old rival and a religion that kept Muslims in mental and political chains. The objection to despotism was not without merit, but Protestant prejudice, with its End Times scenarios, plays into the hands of Muslims who see Americans as latter-day crusaders. Let us recall that the Catholic Crusaders of the Middle Ages sought to recapture Jerusalem from Muslim hands. From an aggrieved Muslim's point of view, the restoration of Jews to the Holy Land, which is a major tenet of Protestant evangelicalism, is not that different. It is, as many Americans and Muslims continue to insist, the same clash of religions that has bedeviled human civilization for millennia.

Humans are driven into clashes of this sort because they have agreed to believe in their own homemade mythologies. And if we agree that, like all things in life, the new often replaces the old, it is rather depressing to see citizens of the American republic and members of Muslim-majority nations holding on to ideas that have long ceased to have any relevance to our realities and are, in fact, plunging our societies and lives into further turmoil and misery. American patriots who proudly wave the stars and banners of their nation ought to recall that the makers of the United States were, to a large extent, critical thinkers affected by the radical philosophies of the Enlightenment in the last three decades of the eighteenth century. Notions like freedom of conscience and self-government were the product of new critical thinking, not revered traditions. The American Revolution marked a turning point in history because it was more a product of the Enlightenment than a new expression of the Christian democracy found in America's earlier sermons. The revolution was not perfect, by any means, but it was still a landmark event. One only imagines what the world would have been—and, in fact, could still be—if the Radical Enlightenment's quest for a "revolution of the mind" had taken place.[59] This revolution would elevate independent thought based on reason over superstition and ancient Middle Eastern tales, eliminate false virtues and markers of identity (such as arbitrarily delineated states), abolish aristocratic tyranny in business and politics, and build economies of common wealth and self-governing societies seeking fraternity.

These are not impossible hopes to have, since many evils of the past have been remedied in the last few centuries. Although racial discrimination is still real for many people today, slavery has long ceased to be legal in the United States and a self-described black man was elected president. Accepting the status quo, however dysfunctional it may be, as a form of hardheaded realism strikes me as an evasive strategy for not having any vision at all. Nations, like individuals, should be judged by their visions, not how they adjust themselves to existing systems. During times of slavery, most people accepted their allotted social roles naturally; only the very few who were alive to the horrors of inhumanity could dream of—and fight for—a different world.

We need more such people now. As was the case with the Declaration of Independence in 1776, we need the strength to distance ourselves from the ideas and ideologies of times and places that no longer suit ours. Defining ourselves in religious, ethnic, or national terms only delays the kind of universalism that motivated enlightened Muslims of the ninth century or the radical European *philosophes* of the late eighteenth. We need to shed light on the many ways we are still governed by biblical tales and prophecies, Islamic traditions that mislead more than they inspire, imagined genealogies that keep us tethered together in strange tribal formations, and a fanatical attachment to land and financial control even when such control ends up controlling our lives more than it liberates us.

What is even more striking is that all our modern knowledge—from great works of literature to groundbreaking scientific discoveries—has done very little to dislodge antiquated ideas. The best we are supposed to do is understand and tolerate modern identities shaped by ancient Middle Eastern men or Mediterranean rulers, not wonder whether such self-understandings have any relevance to our shrunken planet and world community today. Americans and Muslims will not mend their differences fully if they remain enraptured by the ghosts of old religions. Merely understanding our religions, however fabulous they might be, cannot inoculate us against future lapses into the realm of the irrational. Unless we dispatch the prophets of doom that haunt the pages of Semitic scriptures to the pantheon of dead gods, like, say, Greek Zeus, the best we can do is sign truces, not lay the foundations for perpetual peace, one of the unachieved goals of the Enlightenment. As Baron d'Holbach, the eighteenth-century French philosopher of the Enlightenment, put it in 1770: "If error and ignorance have forged the chains which bind peoples in oppression, if it is prejudice which perpetuates those chains, science, reason and truth will one day be able to break them."[60]

Brave men and women tried to act on such principles in eighteenth-century America and France and, as a result, they transformed the world. We inherited the world order they left behind, but we have rarely lived up to their intellectual courage, or matched their bold imagination. We are more comfortable making excuses for our inherited identities than trying to devise healthier ways of inhabiting our age. We could be more passionate about defending our common humanity, instead of waging wars on each other to defend our ethnic groups and artificial nations. We could imagine ourselves as one community confronted by the mistakes of our past and the dangers of the future. We could invest in education as well as health for every living being (human or not) and enrich our lives immeasurably. We could tap into our talents to design a new course for the world, not spend our resources and lives fighting for the ideas, beliefs, and practices that have outlived their usefulness.

So I end where I began. When I look back across the last half millennium, the only event that strikes a blow at all sorts of old regimes is the Declaration that Jefferson wrote to give birth to a new world order. Upon reading it, Europeans abandoned lives of privilege to cross the Atlantic and fight on the side of Americans. The American Revolution it unleashed inspired freedom seekers and poets to imagine a new beginning for the embattled human race. The American, to them, was *Homo universalis*, one who has finally transcended the narrow religious and ethnic differences that had encumbered human progress.

Biblical prophets, however, kept pulling back, and Muslims encountered a conflicted America, not one that had embraced its revolution. Thomas Paine, "America's first modern intellectual," as historian Gordon Wood put it, the first man to use the expression "The United States of America" and who did everything in his power to inspire the birth of the new American republic, was convinced that a new system of government based on freedom would have to be accompanied by the dismantling of the mighty edifice of fables that have come down to us as revealed religions. And such fables to him were not edifying in the least; on the contrary, the holy books of the three monotheistic religions are so full of violence, torture, and debauchery that it would have been more appropriate to see them as the work of the devil. It is, he wrote, "incumbent on every man who reverences the character of the Creator, and who wishes to lessen the catalogue of artificial miseries, and remove the cause that has sown persecutions thick among mankind, to expel all ideas of a revealed religion, as a dangerous heresy, and an impious fraud."[61]

Paine knew that convincing people on such matters was far more perilous than launching an armed revolution against the mightiest empire of the time.[62] The Old Testament proved a mightier rival to Paine's pamphlets and books. Yet our age needs Paine more than it needs Scripture. The legendary veteran of British politics, Michael Foot, attributed the main progressive agenda of his Labour Party to Tom Paine: "International arbitration, family allowances, maternity benefits, free education, prison reform, full employment; much of the future later offered by the British Labour Party was," Foot said, "previously on offer, in better English, from Thomas Paine."[63]

Holiness, as Paine knew, is of our own making. No science tells us that Jerusalem is a better place than Paris, or that Mecca in Saudi Arabia is holier than Tangier. Only religious myths do. And such myths have become dangerous to our twenty-first-century civilization. If we could suspend our religious beliefs for a moment (and certainly put away the negative prejudices that flowed from them) we might have a better chance at paying attention to the future of our common destiny. "It has long been the opinion of the Author," wrote Joel Barlow, the great poet of the American Revolution, "that such a state of peace and happiness as is foretold in scripture and commonly called the millennial period, may rationally be expected to be introduced without a miracle."[64] Western religions have given Americans and Muslims monumental civilizations and rich cultures, ones that we can't imagine our lives without. In fine tuning and revising them to better suit the future, we will only be doing a service to the men (whether real or imagined) who inspired them. Moses, Jesus, and Mohammed, to take the three most obvious examples from the biblical and qur'anic narratives, were prophets because they knew that older ways had ceased to work for their communities. Like America's Founding Fathers, the prophets were men of change, not tradition. All three agreed on the basic principles of love, mercy, and justice, although they charted out paths that suited their own historical circumstances and cultures. By changing the ways to understand religion today we would be honoring the prophetic principle of change, not betraying the spirit of positive religion. Fears of betrayal often lead to ossified practices and dangerous orthodoxies, and this is the last thing we need in our troubled times. We need to fully grasp our relationship to traditional ideas—whether they are religious or nationalistic—before we could envisage a new path for the future. This is why I am not taking the liberty to speculate about how a better world might look like. Because we are still governed by the dictates of the distant past, we must first come to terms with ourselves, each person individually, before we can start a tentative discussion about a workable blueprint for our descendants.

President Obama may not have imagined this herculean struggle with history when, echoing Abraham Lincoln, he warned us that mending the troubled relations between America and Islam requires overcoming our dysfunctional past. The man, after all, is a self-professed Christian. Like some of the Founding Fathers, he surely must know that contesting biblical truths in the United States is a sure recipe for political failure. This is our tragedy. If twenty-first-century Americans cannot speak truth to ancient Middle Eastern power, the hope for Muslims to dispel the fog of the sacred is even slimmer. Until we summon the courage to discuss openly the myths that keep us tethered to an ancient Middle Eastern consciousness, we may not be able to capitalize on the enormous amount of knowledge at our disposal and move forward in any meaningful way. We don't need apocalyptic events in Palestine, rapturous encounters in the sky, and the return to a Golden Age of Islam to fashion a millennium of peace and human solidarity.

Thomas Jefferson, described by the great historian Bernard Bailyn, as "the clear voice of America's Revolutionary ideology, its purest conscience, its most brilliant expositor, [and] its true poet,"[65] imagined a democratic nation without believing in the divine provenance of the Bible. The man, whose principles were described by Abraham Lincoln in 1859 as "the definitions and axioms of free society,"[66] put his trust in human reason—however flawed it may be—not in revelation, however powerful it might sound. But Jefferson, the quintessential American innocent and irrepressible optimist, was a realist, too. Even though he found the violent God of the Hebrews in the Old Testament repugnant, he knew that religion has awesome staying powers. This is why, I suspect, Jefferson didn't spend much time arguing with his fellow citizens about the merits of traditional religion. Instead, he steadfastly defended the civil rights of Jews in the early days of the republic.[67] He did the same for Christians and even Muslims. An enlightened nation stands when it is divided in opinion and faith—however misguided these faiths might be—not when it is united by unproven certitudes. We could all stand to learn from the man who charted the history of modern freedom.

Notes

PREFACE

1. Bernard Lewis, *Faith and Power: Religion and Politics in the Middle East* (New York: Oxford University Press, 2010), 113.

2. Bono, "Rebranding America," *New York Times*, October 18, 2009.

3. Michael B. Oren, *Power, Faith, and Fantasy: America in the Middle East, 1776 to the Present.* (New York: Norton, 2007).

4. Ussama Makdisi, *Faith Misplaced: The Broken Promise of US–Arab Relations: 1820–2001* (New York: PublicAffairs, 2010).

5. Ussama Makdisi, *Artillery of Heaven: American Missionaries and the Failed Conversion of the Middle East* (Ithaca: Cornell University Press, 2008).

6. Fuad Sha'ban, *Islam and Arabs in Early American Thought: The Roots of Orientalism in America* (Durham, NC: Acorn Press, 1990)

7. Fuad Sha'ban, *For Zion's Sake: The Judeo-Christian Tradition in America* (London: Pluto Press, 2005).

8. Timothy Marr, *The Cultural Roots of American Islamicism* (New York: Cambridge University Press, 2006).

9. Thomas S. Kidd, *American Christians and Islam: Evangelical Culture and Muslims from the Colonial Period to the Age of Terrorism* (Princeton: Princeton University Press, 2009).

10. Jonathan Curiel, *Al' America: Travels through America's Arab and Islamic Roots* (New York: The New Press, 2008)

11. Robert J. Allison, *The Crescent Obscured: The United States and the Muslim World, 1776–1815* (New York: Oxford University Press, 1995).

12. Brian Yothers, *The Romance of the Holy Land in American Travel Writing, 1790–1876* (Menston: Scolar Press, 2007).

13. Anouar Majid, "The Political Geography of Holiness," *American Literary History* 21, no. 3 (2009): 633–46.

14. Anouar Majid, "Review of *The Cultural Roots of American Islamicism* by Timothy Marr," *The Historian* 70, no. 1 (Spring 2008): 117–18.

15. Anouar Majid, "Bearing Witness," *Reviews in American History* 37, no. 2 (June 2009): 185–90.

16. Anouar Majid, "Review of *The Crescent Obscured: The United States and the Muslim World, 1776–1815* by Robert J. Allison," *Journal of American Studies of Turkey* (Spring 1998):83–85.

17. Anouar Majid, "Review of *Morocco Bound: Disorienting America's Maghreb, From Casablanca to the Marrakech Express* by Brian Edwards," *Tingis* (2005).

18. Anouar Majid, "Living With Islam," *Chronicle of Higher Education,* March 14, 2003.

19. James A. Field, Jr., *From Gibraltar to the Middle East: America and the Mediterranean World, 1776–1882* (Chicago: Imprint, [1969] 1991).

INTRODUCTION

1. Thomas L. Friedman, "Paging Uncle Sam," *New York Times*, February 25, 2009.

2. Quoted in Fareed Zakaria, *The Post-American World* (New York: Norton, 2008), 234. On the role on America's research universities, see Jonathan R. Cole, *The Great American University: Its Rise to Preeminence, Its Indispensable National Role, Why It Must Be Protected* (New York: PublicAffairs, 2009), 4–5. Although they are about different subjects, both books show why talk of America's decline is premature. On the "brain drain" to the United States, see Maïa de la Baume, "French Fear 'Brain Drain' To the U.S.," *New York Times*, November 22, 2010. On the attraction of American universities to Iranians, see Yeganeh Torbati, "New Wave of Iranians Seek U.S. Studies," *New York Times*, August 10, 2010. On how the humanities separate American education from that of most Asian countries, see Geoffrey Galt Harpham, *The Humanities and the Dream of America* (Chicago: University of Chicago Press, 2011), 150–51. On the reception of the philosopher Michael J. Sander in Asia, see Thomas L. Friedman, "Justice Goes Global," *New York Times*, June 15, 2011. On fraud in Chinese society and higher education, see Andrew Jacobs, "Rampant Fraud Threat to China's Brisk Ascent," *New York Times*, October 6, 2010.

3. Edward Wong, "Photo Turns U.S. Envoy Into a Lesson for Chinese," *New York Times*, August 17, 2011; John F. Burns, "A British Admirer of America Finds His Voice," *New York Times*, August 6, 2011.

4. Ussama Makdisi, *Faith Misplaced: The Broken promise of U.S.–Arab Relations: 1820–2001* (New York: PublicAffairs, 2010).

5. For a transcript of the Tunisia-related cables released by WikiLeaks, see "US Embassy Cables: Tunisia—A US Foreign Policy Conundrum," *Guardian*, http://www.guardian.co.uk/world/us-embassy-cables-documents/217138.

6. For the role the US government and technology companies played in the so-called "Arab Spring," see Mark Landler, "Secret Report Ordered by Obama Identified Potential Uprisings," *New York Times*, February 16, 2011 and Ron Nixon, "U.S. Groups Helped Nurture Arab Uprisings," *New York Times*, April 14, 2011; James Glanz and John Markoff, "U.S. Underwrites Internet Detour Around Censors," *New York Times*, June 13, 2011.

7. http://www.whitehouse.gov/the-press-office/2011/01/14/statement-president-events-tunisia.

8. Scott Shane, "Cables from American Diplomats Portray U.S. Ambivalence on Tunisia," *New York Times*, January 16, 2011; Edward Sklepowich, "In Tunisia: I Have a Dream," Letter to Editor, *New York Times*, January 27, 2011. Obama's statement about the Tunisian uprising was published in "In Quotes: Reaction to the Tunisian Crisis," *BBC News*, January 15, 2011. Mark Landler, "Clinton Gives Scathing Talk on Reform in Arab States," *New York Times*, January 14, 2011; Howard LaFranchi, "Events in Tunisia Bear out Hillary Clinton's Warning to Arab World," *Christian Science Monitor*, January 14, 2011; "Israel: Cable Cites Cooperation Against Hamas," *New York Times*, December 20, 2010. For President Obama's comments on Egypt during his weekly radio address, see http://www.whitehouse.gov/blog/2011/01/28/president-obama-situation-egypt-all-governments-must-maintain-power-through-consent-; David D. Kirkpatrick, "Egypt Erupts in Jubilation as Mubarak Steps Down," *New York Times*, February 11, 2011; Nicholas D. Kristof, "Militants, Women, and Tahrir Sq.," *New York Times*, February 5, 2011.

9. Quoted in Jon Meacham, *American Gospel: God, the Founding Fathers, and the Making of a Nation* (New York: Random House, 2006), 246.

10. See "Remarks by the President at the University of Indonesia in Jakarta, Indonesia," http://www.whitehouse.org, November 10, 2010.

11. Arthur C. Brooks, "Philanthropy and the Non-Profit Sector" in *Understanding America: The Anatomy of an Exceptional Nation*, edited by Peter H. Schuck and James Q. Wilson (New York: Public Affairs, 2008), 542; Stephanie Strom, "Billionaires' Pledge to Give Away Half Gains Followers," *New York Times*, August 5, 2010; Stephanie Storm, "40 Who Committed Half Their Wealth for The Pledge," *New York Times*, November 11, 2010.

12. Michael Barbaro and Javier Hernandez, "Mosque Plan Clears Hurdle in New York," *New York Times*, August 4, 2010; Laurie Goodstein, "Across Nation, Mosque Projects Meet Opposition," *New York Times*, August 7, 2010.

13. Bernard Lewis, *Faith and Power: Religion and Politics in the Middle East* (New York: Oxford University Press, 2010), 81.

14. See Laurie Goodstein, "Poll Finds U.S. Muslims Thriving, but Not Content," *New York Times*, March 2, 2009.

15. For a brief summary of Thomas Danny's career, see http://www.museum.tv/archives/etv/T/htmlT/thomasdanny/thomasdanny.htm.

16. Michael A. Shadid, M.D., *A Doctor for the People: The Autobiography of the Founder of America's First Co-operative Hospital* (New York: Vanguard, 1939). Also see http://digital.library.okstate.edu/encyclopedia/entries/S/SH001.html.

17. Lawrence K. Altman, "The Man on the Table Devised the Surgery," *New York Times*, December 25, 2006; Lawrence K. Altman, "Michael DeBakey. Rebuilder of Hearts, Dies at 99," *New York Times*, July 13, 2008.

18. Denise Grady, "A Conversation with: Elias Zerhouni; Learning the Science of Leading," *New York Times*, July 15, 2003.

19. http://www.radiohof.org/discjockey/caseykasem.html. Mike Hale, "That Casey Kasem Show Was More Than Just Reaching for Stars," *New York Times*, July 8, 2009; Bill Marsh, "Casey Kasem's Velvet-Voiced Countdowns of Summers Past," *New York Times*, July 12, 2009; Pierre Perrone, "Ahmet Ertegün: Founder of Atlantic Records Whose Signings Included Ray Charles, Led Zeppelin and the Rolling Stones," *Independent* (UK), December 16, 2006; Richard Harrington, "The Rhythm of a Heart," *Washington Post*, December 16, 2006; Jon Pareles, "A Mogul Who Helped Mold Pop Culture," *New York Times*, December 16, 2006. For a preview of "Atlantic Records: The House That Ahmet Built," see Virginia Heffernan, "Revealing the Innovator behind the Music," *New York Times*, May 7, 2007.Stephen Kinzer, *Reset: Iran, Turkey, and America's Future* (New York: Times Books, 2010), 87–88.

20. Adam B. Ellick, "Necessity Pushes Pakistani Women Into Jobs and Peril," *New York Times*, December 26, 2010; Brian Knowlton, "Muslim Women Gain Higher Profile in U.S.," *New York Times*, December 27, 2010. For the rankings in Global Gender Report 2010, published by the World Economic Forum, see http://www.weforum.org/reports/global-gender-gap-report-2010?fo=1.

21. Danny Hakim, "Defendant Released in Detroit Terror Case," *New York Times*, October 13, 2004; "Detroit Terror Defendant Released to Halfway House," *Detroit Free Press*, October 13, 2004; "Justices Decide U.S. May Send Two Detainees Back to Algeria," *New York Times*, July 17, 2010.

22. "Justices Decide U.S. May Send Two Detainees Back to Algeria," *New York Times*, July 17, 2010.

23. Dan Eggen, "Gonzales Named to Succeed Ashcroft as Attorney General," *Washington Post*, November 11, 2004; Mike Allen and Jonathan Weisman, "Gutierrez Is Pick for Commerce Secretary," *Washington Post*, November 30, 2004.

24. Christopher Drew, "A Street Cop's Rise from High School Dropout to Cabinet Nominee," *New York Times*, December 3, 2004.
25. Eric Lipton and William K. Rushbaum, "Kerik Pulls Out as Bush Nominee for Homeland Security Job," *New York Times*, December 11, 2004; Joyce Purnik, "Kerik's Friends in High Places, with Blinders," *New York Times*, December 16, 2004; Sam Dolnick, "From Police Commissioner to Prison: Kerik Starts His Four-Year Sentence," *New York Times*, May 17, 2010.
26. Katie Zezma, "The Muslim Patient Will See You Now, Doctor," *New York Times*, September 1, 2004; Maine Medical Center News, "New Hospital Gown Gives Muslim Women Comfort," June 22, 2004, http://www.mmc.org/mmc_news/062204.htm.
27. Barbara Bush, *Reflections: Life after the White House* (New York: Scribner, 2003), ix; Kitty Kelley, *The Family: The Real Story of the Bush Dynasty* (New York: Doubleday, 2004), 127–43.

CHAPTER 1

1. For the full text of the treaty, see http://avalon.law.yale.edu/18th_century/bar1796t.asp.
2. Quotes in John L. Esposito, *The Future of Islam* (New York: Oxford University Press, 2010), 21, 22, 165.
3. Lauren Russell, "Church Plans Quran-burning Event," CNN, July 31, 2010.
4. See Fuad Sha'ban, *For Zion's Sake: The Judeo-Christian Tradition in America* (London: Pluto Press, 2005), 24.
5. Quotes in Timothy Marr, *The Cultural Roots of American Islamicism* (New York: Cambridge University Press, 2006), 1, 97, 103.
6. Robert J. Allison, *The Crescent Obscured: The United States and the Muslim World, 1776–1815* (New York: Oxford University Press, 1995), 47.
7. Thomas S. Kidd, *American Christians and Islam: Evangelical Culture and Muslims from the Colonial Period to the Age of Terrorism* (Princeton: Princeton University Press, 2009), 11.
8. Quoted in Kidd, *American Christians and Islam*, 6.
9. Marr, *The Cultural Roots of American Islamicism*, 23.
10. Quoted in Kidd, *American Christians and Islam*, 20.
11. Quoted in Sha'ban, *For Zion's Sake*, 66.
12. Quoted in ibid., 67.
13. Frank Lambert, *The Barbary Wars: American Independence in the Atlantic World* (New York: Hill and Wang, 2005), 110.
14. Marr, *The Cultural Roots of American Islamicism*, 39.
15. Lambert, *The Barbary Wars*, 112.

16. Paul Johnson, "The Answer to Terrorism? Colonialism," *Wall Street Journal*, October 9, 2001.

17. Quoted in Allison, *The Crescent Obscured*, 205–06. For a history of Francis Scott Key and "The Star-Spangled Banner," see http:www.usflag.org/francis.scott.key.html.

18. Quoted in Marr, *The Cultural Roots of American Islamicism*, 207.

19. Quoted in Sha'ban, *For Zion's Sake*, 50.

20. Quoted in ibid., 37.

21. Ussama Makdisi, *Artillery of Heaven: American Missionaries and the Failed Conversion of the Middle East* (Ithaca: Cornell University Press, 2008), 43.

22. Ibid., 70–71, 72–73.

23. Ibid., 146.

24. Ibid., 95–96, 99.

25. Quoted in Michael B. Oren, *Power, Faith, and Fantasy: America in the Middle East, 1776 to the Present* (New York: Norton, 2007), 214.

26. Quoted in Kidd, *American Christians and Islam*, 52.

27. Kidd, *American Christians and Islam*, 53–54.

28. Quoted in Fuad Sha'ban, *Islam and Arabs in Early American Thought: The Roots of Orientalism in America* (Durham: The Acorn Press, in association with Duke University Islamic and Arabian Development Studies, 1991), 94–95.

29. Kidd, *American Christians and Islam*, 43–44.

30. Ibid., 48–50. Henry Jessup was remarkably well informed about the status of women in Arab and Muslim cultures. His book, *The Woman of the Arabs*, first published in 1873, has been reissued, complete and unabridged, in 2008 by Tutis Digital Publishing Private Limited.

31. Ibid., 59.

32. Ibid., 58–71.

33. Ibid., 65–77.

34. Ibid., 122, 128.

35. Ibid., 147, 150, 163.

CHAPTER 2

1. For extracts on Luther's statements, visit the Jewish Virtual Library at http://www.jewishvirtuallibrary.org/jsource/anti-semitism/Luther_on_Jews.html.

2. Quoted in Regina S. Sharif, *Non-Jewish Zionism: Its Roots in Western History* (London: Zed Press, 1983), 24.

3. Ibid., 28.

4. Quoted in Dan Cohn-Sherbok, *The Politics of Apocalypse: The History and Influence of Christian Zionism* (Oxford, UK: Oneworld Publications, 2006), 26–27.

5. Sharif, *Non-Jewish Zionism*, 33–49, 50–51, 71; Theodor Herzl, *The Jewish State* (New York: Dover Publications, 1988), 69.

6. Shalom Goldman, *Zeal for Zion: Christians, Jews, and the Idea of the Promised Land* (Chapel Hill: University of North Carolina Press, 2009), 22–23.

7. Quoted in Cohn-Sherbok, *The Politics of Apocalypse*, 76.

8. Quoted in Goldman, *Zeal for Zion*, 23.

9. James A. Field, Jr., *From Gibraltar to the Middle East: America and the Mediterranean World, 1776–1882* (Chicago: Imprint Publications, [1969] 1991), 79.

10. Eitan Bar-Yosef, *The Holy Land in English Culture, 1799–1917* (Oxford, UK: Clarendon Press, 2005), 262.

11. Donald M. Lewis, *The Origins of Christian Zionism: Lord Shaftesbury and Evangelical Support for a Jewish Homeland* (New York: Cambridge University Press, 2010), 331–33.

12. Sharif, *Non-Jewish Zionism*, 76. Montagu's memorandum on the anti-Semitism of the Balfour Declaration can be found at http://www.jewish virtuallibrary.org/jsource/History/Montagumemo.htmla.

13. Field, *From Gibraltar to the Middle East*, 281–82.

14. Quoted in Timothy Marr, *The Cultural Roots of American Islamicism* (New York: Cambridge University Press, 2006), 85.

15. "John Adams Embraces a Jewish Homeland" in http://www.ajhs.org /scholarship/chapters/chapter.cfm?documentID=221.

16. Field, *From Gibralter to the Middle East*, 277–79; Michael B. Oren, *Power, Faith, and Fantasy: America in the Middle East, 1776 to the Present* (New York: Norton, 2007), 141.

17. Quoted in Brian Yothers, *The Romance of the Holy Land in American Travel Writing, 1790–1876* (Burlington: Ashgate, 2007), 50.

18. Field, *From Gibraltar to the Middle East*, 276–77, 279–80; Yothers, *The Romance of the Holy Land in American Travel Writing*, 53.

19. Quoted in Sha'ban, *For Zion's Sake*, 82.

20. Quoted in ibid., 92.

21. Quoted in ibid., 93.

22. Quoted in ibid., 132–33.

23. Quoted in ibid., 138.

24. Quoted in Oren, *Power, Faith, and Fantasy*, 221.

25. Oren, *Power, Faith, and Fantasy*, 273–75.

26. Goldman, *Zeal for Zion*, 24–26.

27. Oren, *Power, Faith, and Fantasy*, 359.

28. Ibid., 351–62.

29. Donald M. Lewis, *The Origins of Christian Zionism: Lord Shaftes-bury and Evangelical Support for a Jewish Homeland* (New York: Cambridge University Press, 2010), 21.

30. Oren, *Power, Faith, and Fantasy*, 362–63.

31. Quoted in Oren, *Power, Faith, and Fantasy*, 364.

32. Oren, *Power, Faith, and Fantasy*, 390.

33. Quoted in ibid., 427.

34. Quoted in ibid., 435.

35. Quoted in ibid., 437.

36. Oren, *Power, Faith, and Fantasy*, 438–45.

37. Quoted in Oren, *Power, Faith, and Fantasy*, 455.

38. Ibid., 471–72.

39. Kidd, *American Christians and Islam*, 80–81, 83.

40. Ibid., 86–87, 91.

41. Quoted in Oren, *Power, Faith, and Fantasy*, 484.

42. Oren, *Power, Faith, and Fantasy*, 484–501.

43. Ibid., 91–92.

44. This is how the first American missionaries to the Middle East described their enterprise in Boston on the eve of their departure in November 1819. Pliny Fisk dreamed of "spiritual conquests" while his colleague and friend, Levi Parsons, was gearing up for a "spiritual crusade." See Ussama Makdisi, *Faith Misplaced: The Broken Promise of US–Arab Relations: 1820–2001* (New York: PublicAffairs, 2010), 24, 109.

45. Sharif, *Non-Jewish Zionism*, 90–119.

46. Lewis, *The Origins of Christian Zionism*, 21.

47. Sharif, *Non-Jewish Zionism*, 94.

48. Sha'ban, *For Zion's Sake*, 159–60.

49. Shalom Goldman, "Oral Roberts, Pioneering Christian Zionist," *Religion Dispatches*, January 10, 2010.

50. Cohn-Sherbok, *The Politics of Apocalypse*, 162.

51. Quoted in Sha'ban, *For Zion's Sake*, 156.

52. Shalom Goldman, "Huckabee in the Holy Land: A Christian Zionist Campaign," *Religion Dispatches*, September 20, 2009.

CHAPTER 3

1. Quoted in Paul Baepler, "The Barbary Captivity Narrative in Early America," *Early American Literature* 30, no. 2 (1995): 113.

2. Quoted in Lotfi Ben Rejeb, "American's Captive Freeman in North Africa: The Comparative Method in Abolitionist Persuasion," *Slavery and Abolition* 9, no. 1 (1988): 61, 62.

3. Robert J. Allison, *The Crescent Obscured: The United States and the Muslim World, 1776–1815* (New York: Oxford University Press, 1995), 101.

4. William Wilshire Riley, *Sequel to Riley's Narrative: Being a Sketch of Interesting Incidents in the Life, Voyage and Travels of Capt. James Riley. . .* (Columbus: George Brewster, 1851), 387–88.

5. James Riley, *An Authentic Narrative of the Loss of the American Brigg Commerce, Wrecked on the Western Coast of Africa, in the Month of August, 1815 . . .* (New York: Riley, 1817), 250–51.

6. For a facsimile of George Washington's letter, see http://mideasti. blogapot.com/2011/07/for-fourth-first-to-recognize-us.html.

7. See R. Grald McMurty, "The Influence of Riley's *Narrative* upon Abraham Lincoln," *Indiana Magazine of History*, June 1934, 133–38.

8. Royall Tyler, *The Algerine Captive, Or, The Life and Adventures of Doctor Updike Underhill: Six Years a Prisoner Among the Algerines* (New York: Modern Library, 2002), 183.

9. Ibid., 226.

10. Hilton Obenzinger, *American Palestine: Melville, Twain, and the Holy Land Mania* (Princeton: Princeton University Press, 1999), xi.

11. Quotes in Brian Yothers, *The Romance of the Holy Land in American Travel Writing, 1790–1876* (Burlington: Ashgate, 2007), 115, 120.

12. Ibid., 132.

13. Quoted in Jonathan Curiel, *Al' America: Travels through America's Arab and Islamic Roots* (New York: The New Press, 2008), 43.

14. Curiel, *Al' America*, 43–44, 50–51.

15. Quoted in ibid., 43–44.

16. Ralph Waldo Emerson, "The Preacher," in *The Complete Works of Ralph Waldo Emerson: Vol. 10: Lectures and Biographical Sketches (Boston: Houghton, Mifflin and Company, 1904), 226–27.*

17. Quoted in Curiel, *Al' America*, 44–45.

18. James A. Field, Jr., *From Gibraltar to the Middle East: America and the Mediterranean World, 1776–1882* (Chicago: Imprint Publications, [1969] 1991), 251.

19. Curiel, *Al' America*, 145–54.

20. Ibid., 116.

21. Quoted in Susan Nance, *How the Arabian Nights Inspired the American Dream, 1790–1935* (Chapel Hill: University of North Carolina Press, 2009), 105.

22. Curiel, *Al' America*, 83–104.

23. Ibid., 2, 3, 67.

24. Jonathan Lyons, *The House of Wisdom: How the Arabs Transformed Western Civilization* (New York: Bloomsbury, 2009), 1–6.

25. Ibid., 26, 40.

26. Ibid., 63.

27. Ibid., 111.

28. Ibid., 121–22.

29. Quoted in Matthew Carr, *Blood and Faith: The Purging of Muslim Spain* (New York: The New Press, 2009), 19.

30. Quoted in John L. Esposito, *The Future of Islam* (New York: Oxford University Press, 2010), 170.

31. Curiel, *Al' America*, 131–44.

32. Ibid., 167.

33. Franklin D. Lewis, *Rumi: Past and Present, East and West: The Life, Teaching, and Poetry of Jalâl al-Din Rumi* (Oxford: Oneworld Publications, 2000), 1–37.

34. Terry Pristin, "Bringing the Mall of America Magic to New Jersey," *New York Times*, May 10, 2011.

35. Mark Twain, *Innocents Abroad, or The New Pilgrims' Progress*, facsimile edition (New York: Hoppocrene Books, undated), 368.

CHAPTER 4

1. Quoted in Michael B. Oren, *Power, Faith, and Fantasy: America in the Middle East, 1776 to the Present* (New York: Norton, 2007), 125.

2. Quoted in ibid., 130.

3. Ibid., 130–37; James A. Field, Jr., *From Gibraltar to the Middle East: America and the Mediterranean World, 1776–1882* (Chicago: Imprint Publications, [1969] 1991), 189, 190, 249.

4. Field, *From Gibraltar to the Middle East*, 154–56, 159, 243, 188.

5. Ibid., 385–88.

6. Ibid., 389–435.

7. Oren, *Power, Faith, and Fantasy*, 207.

8. Ted Widmer, *Ark of Liberties: America and the World* (New York: Hill and Wang, 2008), 143–44. Reverend Cyrus Hamlin was a graduate of two Maine institutions: Bowdoin College and Bangor Theological Seminary. Field describes him as "a shatterer of precedent." Field, *From Gibraltar to the Middle East*, 352.

9. See the website of Robert College at http://portal.robcol.k12.tr. On the relationship between Robert College and the birth of a Turkish nation, see Field, *From Gibraltar to the Middle East*, 359.

10. See the website of AUB at http://www.aub.edu.lb. Bliss is quoted in Ussama Makdisi, *Faith Misplaced: The Broken Promise of US–Arab Relations: 1820–2001* (New York: PublicAffairs, 2010), 53.

11. Quoted in Oren, *Power, Faith, and Fantasy*, 218.

12. Field, *From Gibraltar to the Middle East*, 350.

13. Oren, *Power, Faith, and Fantasy*, 285.

14. Ibid., 285–90.

15. Ibid., 228, 231.

16. Quoted in ibid., 237.

17. Ibid., 238.

18. Ibid., 249–53.

19. Ibid., 270.

20. Makdisi, *Faith Misplaced*, 79–80; also, see 57, 61, 63–65. In his book, *The Arab Awakening* (1938), George Antonius acknowledged the American missionaries' contribution to the making of an Arab consciousness. See Makdisi, *Faith Misplaced*, 177.

21. See, for instance, Elizabeth Boosahda, *Arab-American Faces and Voices: The Origins of an Immigrant Community* (Austin: University of Texas Press, 2003).

22. For an excellent account of the history of Syrian immigration to the United States, see Sarah M. A. Gualtieri, *Between Arab and White: Race and Ethnicity in the Early Syrian American Diaspora* (Berkeley: University of California Press, 2009).

23. Sayyid Qutb, "'The America I Have Seen': In the Scale of Human Values," in *America in an Arab Mirror: Images of America in Arabic Travel Literature*, ed. Kamal Abdel-Malek, trans. Tarek Masoud and Ammar Fakeeh (New York: St. Martin's Press, 2000), 9-27.

24. Quoted in ibid., 54.

25. Quoted in Suheil B. Bushrui, "The Thought and Works of Ameen Rihani" at http://www.alhewar.com/Bushrui_Rihani.html.

26. Quoted in Waïl Hassan, "The Rise of Arab-American Literature: Orientalism and Cultural Translation in the Work of Ameen Rihani," *American Literary History* 20 (1–2): 258.

27. Both long quotations are from The Project Gutenberg EBook of *The Book of Khalid*, by Ameen Rihani, available at http://www.gutenberg .org/ebooks/29257.

28. Quoted in Gualtieri, *Between Arab and White*, 96.

29. Abraham Mitrie Rihbany, *America Save the Middle East* (Boston: The Beacon Press, 1918), 26, 85, 101–24, 135–37, 142, 145, 157.

30. Quoted in Gualtieri, *Between Arab and White*, 93.

31. Michael A. Shadid, *A Doctor for the People: The Autobiography of the Founder of America's First Co-Operative Hospital* (New York: Vanguard, 1939), 26–28.

32. Salom Rizk, *Syrian Yankee* (Garden City: Doubleday, 1943).

33. See Gualtieri, *Between Arab and White*.

34. Field, *From Gibraltar to the Middle East*, 310; Graham H. Stuart, "The Future of Tangier," *Foreign Affairs* 23, no. 4 (July 1945): 675. Stuart wrote that the sultan's intention was recorded in documents archived at the American Legation, but which, according to Gerald Lotfus, the Legation director

in 2011, have yet to be identified. See Gerald Lotfus's blog entry, "History Tantalizingly Within Reach," www.talimblog.com, May 25, 2011.

35. See Walter A. McDougall, *Freedom Just Around the Corner: A New American History 1585–1828* (New York: HarperCollins, 2004).

36. Renata Adler, "The Screen: Zane Grey Meets the Marquis de Sade," *New York Times*, January 25, 1968.

37. See Peter B. Flint, "Sergio Leone, 67, Italian Director Who Revitalized Western, Dies," *New York Times*, May 1, 1989.

38. Walter A. McDougall, *Promised Land, Crusader State: The American Encounter with the World Since 1776* (Boston: Houghton Mifflin, 1997), 1–2.

39. Christopher Frayling, *Once Upon a Time in America: The Westerns of Sergio Leone* (New York: Harry N. Abrams, 2005), 20.

40. Abby Goodnough, "160 Acres of Mosquitoes and Dust? To Him, Priceless," *New York Times*, June 13, 2004; "Man in Everglades Accepts State Buyout," *New York Times*, April 14, 2005.

41. H. L. Mencken, *The American Language: An Inquiry into the Development of English in the United States*, 2nd ed., revised and enlarged (New York: A. A. Knopf, 1921), 263.

42. Field, *From Gibraltar to the Middle East*, 452 – 53.

43. Ibid., 358.

44. Quoted in ibid., 350–51.

45. Quoted in ibid., 427.

46. Ibid., 450–52.

47. Ibid., 102.

48. Stephen Kinzer, *Reset: Iran, Turkey, and America's Future* (New York: Times Books, 2010), 22.

CHAPTER 5

1. Nicholas Kulish, "Obama Gets High Marks Abroad, Survey Finds," *New York Times*, June 18, 2010; Charles M. Blow, "The Thrill Is Gone," *New York Times*, June 19, 2010. For a brief report on the University of Maryland/Zogby poll, see "Survey: Arabs Lose Faith in Obama," *Aljazeera .net*, August 6, 2010; Norimitsu Onishi, "In Jakarta Speech, Some Hear Cairo Redux," *New York Times*, November 10, 2010.

2. For more on a critical reading of the Qur'an, see Mondher Sfar, *In Search of the Original Koran: The True History of the Revealed Text*, trans. Emilia Lanier (Amherst: Prometheus Books, 2008).

3. See Abdelwahab Meddeb, *Pari de Civilisation* (Paris: Éditions du Seuil, 2009), 137.

4. Abdullahi Ahmed An-Na'im, *Islam and the Secular State: Negotiating the Future of Shari'a* (Cambridge: Harvard University Press, 2008), 34, 12, 282–83.

5. Hans Küng, *Islam: Past, Present, and Future*, translated from German by John Bowden (Oxford: Oneworld, 2007), 111. Küng's book offers an excellent intellectual history of Islam from its inception to our times.

6. For an excellent account of the first decade after the Prophet's death, see Lesley Hazleton, *After the Prophet: The Epic Story of the Shia—Sunni Split in Islam* (New York: Doubleday, 2009).

7. "Arab Democracy: A Commodity Still in Short Supply," *Economist*, December 2, 2010.

8. Samuel M. Zwemer, *The Disintegration of Islam* (New York: Fleming H. Revell Company, 1916), 8–49.

9. Ibid., 89.

10. Ibid., 142–43.

11. Dan Diner, *Lost in the Sacred: Why the Muslim World Stood Still*, translated from German by Steven Rendall (Princeton: Princeton University Press, 2009), 13. I am grateful to Professor Joel Gordon of the University of Arkansas who brought this book to my attention.

12. *Arab Human Development Report 2003: Building a Knowledge Society*, http://hdr.undp.org/en/reports/regionalreports/arabstates/arab_states_2003_en.pdf, 127.

13. Diner, *Lost in the Sacred*, 80, 83.

14. Ibid., 88.

15. Ibid., 155.

16. Ibid., 161.

17. Ibid., 158, 164.

18. Ibid., 9, 167.

19. Ibid., 165–80.

20. Quoted in Küng, *Islam*, 468.

21. F. E. Peters, *The Voice, the Word, the Books: The Sacred Scripture of the Jews, Christians, and Muslims* (Princeton: Princeton University Press, 2007), 3.

22. For a fascinating study of the culture of power in Muslim Arab lands, see Lawrence Rosen, *Varieties of Muslim Experience: Encounters with Arab Political and Cultural Life* (Chicago: University of Chicago Press, 2008).

23. Vali Nasr, *Forces of Fortune: The Rise of the New Muslim Middle Class and What It Will Mean for our World* (New York: Free Press, 2009).

24. Ibid., 260.

25. David Gardner, *Last Chance: The Middle East in the Balance* (London: I. B. Tauris, 2009).

26. Ibid., 28, 33.

27. Landon Thomas Jr., "Turkey Prospers by Turning East," *New York Times*, July 6, 2010.

28. Gardner, *Last Chance*, 202.

29. Adm. Mike Mullen, "Strategic Communication: Getting Back to Basics,"*Joint Chiefs of Staff*, August 28, 2009, http://www.jcs.mil/news article.aspx?ID=142.

CHAPTER 6

1. David Armitage, *The Declaration of Independence: A Global History* (Cambridge, MA: Harvard University Press, 2007), 30. The quote from Jefferson is one page 21.

2. James A. Field, Jr., *From Gibraltar to the Middle East: America and the Mediterranean World, 1776–1882* (Chicago: Imprint Publications, [1969] 1991), 8.

3. Ibid., 9–13.

4. Armitage, *The Declaration of Independence*, 13, 3, 134.

5. Ibid., 112–13.

6. Quoted in ibid., 62.

7. Quoted in Jacques M. Wendel, "Turgot and the American Revolution," *Modern Age* (Summer 1979): 284.

8. Quoted in Armitage, *The Declaration of Independence*, 108–9.

9. Quoted in ibid., 15.

10. Field, *From Gibraltar to the Middle East*, 214.

11. Ted Widmer, *Ark of Liberties: America and the World* (New York: Hill and Wang, 2008), 96.

12. Quoted in Armitage, *The Declaration of Independence*, 1.

13. Abraham Lincoln to Henry L. Pierce, April 6, 1859, http://showcase. netins.net/web/creative/lincoln/speeches/pierce.htm; quoted in Armitage, *The Declaration of Independence*, 97.

14. Widmer, *Ark of Liberties*, 99.

15. Quoted in ibid., 105–06.

16. Ibid., 118–20.

17. Quoted in ibid., 129.

18. Quoted in ibid., 171.

19. Quoted in ibid., 179.

20. Ibid., 181–86.

21. Ibid., 204, 210–11.

22. Ibid., 216.

23. Ibid., 220–21.

24. Ibid., 241–42.

25. Stephen Kinzer, *Reset: Iran, Turkey, and America's Future* (New York: Times Books, 2010), 97.

26. Widmer, *Ark of Liberties*, 266, 269–70.

27. Quoted in Kinzer, *Reset*, 110.

28. Quoted in Kinzer, *Reset*, 123.

29. The expression was used by President George W. Bush during the State of the Union Address on January 29, 2002. The speech is available at http://georgewbush-whitehouse.archives.gov/news/releases/2002/01/print/20020129-11.html.

30. Kinzer, *Reset*, 103.

31. William Greider, *Come Home, America: The Rise and Fall (and Redeeming Promise) of Our Country* (New York: Rodale, 2009).

32. University of Michigan, Collected Works of Abraham Lincoln, Vol. 5; available at http://quod.lib.umich.edu/l/lincoln/lincoln5/1:87?rgn=div1;view=fulltext.

33. Norimitsu Onishi, "U.S. Updates The Brand It Promotes In Indonesia," *New York Times*, March 6, 2011.

34. Thomas L. Friedman, "Pharaoh without a Mummy," *New York Times*, February 16, 2011; Thomas L. Friedman, "The $110 Billion Question," *New York Times*, March 6, 2011.

35. Ameen Rihani, *The Fate of Palestine* (Beirut, Lebanon: The Rihani Printing & Publishing House, 1967), 27.

36. Michel Abitbol, *Le passé d'une discorde: Juifs et Arabes depuis le VII siècle* (Paris, France: Perrin, 2003), 240; Ameen Rihani, *The Fate of Palestine* (Beirut, Lebanon: The Rihani Printing & Publishing House, 1967), 14–40. Denouncing anti-Semitism at every turn and favoring the cultural contributions of the Jews to the region, Rihani believed that political Zionism heralded an endless future of strife and conflict.

37. Martin Gilbert, *In Ishmael's House: A History of Jews in Muslim Lands* (New Haven: Yale University Press, 2010).

38. Isabel Kershner, "Drive for Palestinian Unity Exposes Fractured Society," *New York Times*, May 6, 2011; Nicholas D. Kristoff, "In Israel, The Noble Vs. The Ugly," *New York Times*, July 8, 2010; Bernard Lewis, *Faith and Power: Religion and Politics in the Middle East* (New York: Oxford University Press, 2010), 202.

39. See Donald Snyder, "In Germany, Jews Fight Wave of Islamophobia Even as Some Muslims Denounce Jews," *Forward*, January 14, 2011.

40. Michael Abitol, *Le passé d'une discorde: Juifs et Arabes depuis le VII siècle* (Paris, France: Perrin, 2003), 250.

41. *The Israel–Arab Reader: A Documentary History of the Middle East Conflict*, eds. Walter Laqueur and Barry Rubin, 7th & updated edition (New York: Penguin Books, 2008), 17.

42. *The Israel–Arab Reader*, 19.

43. Abitbol, *Le passé d'une discorde*, 250; Gilbert, *In Ishmael's House*, 147–48, 172–73. See *The Israel-Arab Reader: A Documentary History of the Middle East Conflict*, eds. Walter Laqueur and Barry Rubin, seventh and updated edition (New York: Penguin Books, 2008), 9, 17–21.

44. Salom Rizk, *Syrian Yankee* (Garden City, NY: Doubleday, 1943), 259, 261.

45. See Dan Senor and Saul Singer, *Start-Up Nation: The Story of Israel's Miracle* (New York: Twelve, 2009); Dina Kraft, "Where Families Are Prized, Help Is Free," *New York Times*, July 18, 2011. For a list of brief facts on Israel, visit Israel's Ministry of Foreign Affairs site at http://www.mfa.gov.il/mfa/facts about israel/israel in brief.

46. "New Potato Variety to be Irrigated with Salt Water," *Greenmed Journal*, July 16, 2010; Amiram Cohen, "Israeli Company Develops Tomato That Doesn't Need to Be Refrigerated," *Haaretz*, August 24, 2010.

47. Ussama Makdisi, *Faith Misplaced: The Broken Promise of US–Arab Relations: 1820–2001* (New York: PublicAffairs, 2010), 210–12.

48. Ethan Bronner, "After a Loss, a Father Sees a Lesson for Palestinians in a Translation of an Israeli's Work," *New York Times*, March 6, 2010.

49. Lewis, *Faith and Power*, 54.

50. See Alain Gresh, "Un seul Etat pour deux rêves," *Le Monde diplomatique*, October 2010.

51. *The Israel-Arab Reader*, 82–83.

52. See Israel Finkelstein and Neil Asher Silberman, *The Bible Unearthed: Archaeology's New Vision of Ancient Israel and the Origin of Its Sacred Texts* (New York: Touchstone, 2002).

53. Basem L. Ra'ad, *Hidden Histories: Palestine and the Eastern Mediterranean* (London: Pluto Press, 2010), 70.

54. Quoted in ibid., 75.

55. Ibid., 75–76; Stephen Sizer, *Christian Zionism: Road-map to Armageddon?* (Downers Grove: IVP Academic, 2004), 234–53; Isabel Kershner, "Israel Chafes as Palestinian Denies Its Link to Western Wall," *New York Times*, November 26, 2010; James Hider, "A Tragic Misunderstanding," *Times of London*, January 13, 2009.

56. Slavoj Zizek, "Let Jerusalem Go," Letter to Editor, *London Review of Books*, 28, no. 16 (August 17, 2006).

57. Juan Cole, *Engaging the Muslim World* (New York: Palgrave Macmillan, 2009), 5.

58. Gary Gerstle, *American Crucible: Race and Nation in the Twentieth Century* (Princeton: Princeton University Press, 2001).

59. Jonathan Israel, *A Revolution of the Mind: Radical Enlightenment and the Intellectual Origins of Modern Democracy* (Princeton: Princeton University Press, 2010).

60. Quoted in ibid., 36.

61. Thomas Paine, *The Age of Reason, Being an Investigation of True and Fabulous Theology,* in Paine: *Collected Writings* (New York: Library of America, 1995), 822; Gordon S. Wood, *Revolutionary Characters: What Made the Founders Different* (New York: Penguin Books, 2006), 218.

62. Paine, *The Age of Reason,* 665, 731.

63. Quoted in Craig Nelson, *Thomas Paine: Enlightenment, Revolution, and the Birth of Modern Nations* (New York: Viking, 2006), 333.

64. Quoted in Field, *From Gibraltar to the Middle East,* 15.

65. Quoted in Nelson, *Thomas Paine,* 98.

66. Abraham Lincoln to Henry L. Pierce, April 6, 1859, http://showcase.netins.net/web/creative/lincoln/speeches/pierce.htm.

67. For a wonderful portrait of Jefferson as an eighteenth-century Enlightenment figure, see Wood, *Revolutionary Characters,* 91–117. On "Jefferson and the Jews," see http://www.ajhs.org/scholarship/chapters/chapter.cfm?documentID=219.

Index

About the Author

Anouar Majid is author of several critically acclaimed books on Islam and the West, including *A Call for Heresy* and *We are All Moors*. His work has been featured in the *Bill Moyers Journal* and Al Jazeera television. Majid is director of the Center for Global Humanities and associate provost for Global Initiatives at the University of New England.